THE MENTAL HEALTH PRESCRIPTION

Personalized Exercise and Nutrition Strategies for Bulletproof Mental Health

By

IGOR KLIBANOV

Igor Klibanov

Copyright©2021 by Igor Klibanov

ISBN: 979-8-7396943-2-4

All rights reserved. No part of this publication may be reproduced; stored in a retrieval system, or transmitted in any form or by any means, electronics, mechanical, photocopying, recording, or otherwise, without the prior written permission of the publisher.

CONTENTS

Acknowledgements 7

Introduction 10

Exercise for Anxiety 17

> What is anxiety (diagnostic criteria)... What's better – cardio or strength training?... Why exercising with high intensity might actually make your anxiety worse... The least amount of exercise you can do and still experience anxiety relief... The number of days per week necessary for exercise to work to reduce anxiety... exercise vs. medications – what works better?... 4 mechanisms by which exercise decreases anxiety... How to figure out what works FOR YOU

Exercise Induced Panic Attack 37

> The surprising similarities between exercise and panic attacks... 5 strategies to reduce or avoid panic attacks during exercise... How to warm up properly for people suffering from exercise-induced panic attacks (and how it's different than for people who don't have it)...Two simple (but effective) questions that will take the "edge" off future panic

attacks... How to reduce your panic attacks 5 minutes at a time

Exercise for Depression 45

What is depression (diagnostic criteria)... What's better – cardio or strength training (hint: it's not the same as for anxiety)... How many days per week you need to exercise for depression relief... The necessary intensity of exercise for improvements in depression... Why the length of time that you exercise isn't that important, and what is important... How exercise compares to medications... 3 strategies to get a depressed person to exercise in the first place

Exercise for PTSD 62

The exercise prescription for PTSD – type (cardio vs. strength training vs. stretching), duration, and frequency

How to Individualize (Questionnaire) 66

The 30-second questionnaire that will help you figure out the perfect exercise prescription FOR YOU... the importance of testing different forms of exercise... How to systematically test different variables (intensity, duration, type, etc.) to figure out what's right for you.

Mechanisms: Why Exercise Improves Mental Health 70

7 ways by which exercise improves mental health

Nutrition for Anxiety 74

The 2 most common conditions confused with anxiety – are you getting the wrong treatment?... Is your thyroid health undermining your mental health?... Why low blood sugar may sometimes be confused for anxiety... Why it's so hard to diagnose low blood sugar... Is your coffee addiction contributing to your anxiety?... Could this common artificial sweetener be making your anxiety worse?... Are your "gut bacteria" anxious?... How to figure out if your mental health issues are related to poor digestion... The 4R program to improve digestion... The inflammation connection... How inflammation affects the brain, to cause anxiety... 4 strategies for reducing inflammation... 4 supplements that may improve your anxiety

Nutrition for Depression 102

The 2 most common conditions confused with anxiety – are you getting the wrong treatment?... Is your thyroid health undermining your mental health?... Why low blood sugar may sometimes be confused for depression... Why it's so hard to diagnose low blood sugar... The difference between food allergies and food sensitivities... how food sensitivities can contribute to depression... The inflammation connection… How inflammation affects the brain, to cause anxiety… 4 strategies for reducing inflammation… Why alcohol makes depression better in the short term, but worse in the long term… How MSG sensitivity can make depression worse… The 3 supplements that can improve depression… The 2 nutrients that if they're deficient can cause depression-like symptoms, and supplementing with them will remove those symptoms

Conclusion and Quick Reference Guide 86

Go here if you don't want to read the theory, and just want to be told what to do

References 130

Acknowledgements

In this section, I would like to acknowledge and thank the people without whom this book would have been complete, unintelligible gibberish. These people helped with editing, making the text easy-to-read, and suggested which illustrations to include. In no particular order:

- Chris Sousa: he's the fitness officer and athletic coordinator at Seneca College, and a beast of an athlete in his own right. From competing in powerlifting, to weightlifting, to even a half marathon, he's the real deal. And one of the kindest people I know.
- Krysta Leoness: she's a nutritionist, tantrika and author of *Awakening the Yoni*
- Lyn Chen is a savvy entrepreneur, and current co-owner of an edible utensil company called "Candy Cutlery"
- Raymond Wong is a Certified Holistic Nutritionist, who also studies Energy Healing
- Aleks Wojcik is a fellow Personal Trainer and Holistic Nutritionist. Her own struggles led her to research and study mental health and its connection to nutrition and the digestive system. Consequently, she became a Nutritionist who

specializes in digestive health. In turn, adding her perspective to this book.

- Daman Singh is a long-time friend of mine, who I met at Seneca College. A man of many talents. He's played basketball, competed in powerlifting, and now, dancing as a popper (if you don't know what that is – youtube it!).
- Disha Alam is a friend who works as a midwife. She's currently working on her Master's.
- Henry Korenblum is a long-time friend of mine. He works as a Business Succession Specialist, and despite a busy family with a wife and 2 young kids, he was able to kindly contribute his time to editing this book.
- Ella Levin is a friend of mine who works in finance. Alongside her mathematical inclination, she is very meticulous when it comes to punctuation and sentence structure.
- Richie Binzangi is a fellow personal trainer, as well as powerlifter.
- George Stavrou is both a friend and former client who has decades of experience in the fitness/nutrition industry, and now, runs a comprehensive online health program called "The Stavrou Method." You can check it out by visiting https:// thestavroumethod.com/

- Dr. Romi Fung is a Naturopathic Physician in Richmond, British Columbia. He has extensive knowledge in mental health and has clinical interests in treating Alzheimer's Disease and Dementia

Introduction

You probably picked up this book because you're struggling with mental health. Maybe it's anxiety, maybe it's depression, PTSD, or something else. Or perhaps, you have friends or family members with these conditions. Or perhaps you're a health/fitness professional, wanting to help your clients or patients.

If so, then this book is for you.

You, your friend, family member or client(s) has been struggling with a mental health issue, and you keep hearing that "exercise is good for you." But you're not really sure exactly <u>what</u> to do.

I mean, when a doctor prescribes a medication, there is a lot of precision behind it. You know:

- The name of the medication.
- The dosage.
- Whether it should be taken with food or without food, and
- Whether it should be taken in the morning, noon or evening

But when the doctor recommends exercise, well, the recommendation is vague. You don't know exactly how to do it. You need the exercise prescription for different conditions. To know the exercise prescription you need to know:

- The **type** of exercise, such as: cardio, strength training, or stretching

- The **frequency**: how many days per week you should exercise. It's not always a "more is better" type of scenario. With some things there's a "sweet spot", where too little is not stimulating, and too much is implausible. The "sweet spot" varies condition-by-condition, and person-to-person

- The **duration**: how long you should exercise for

- The **intensity**: at what percent of your maximal effort do you exercise?

Just as a doctor does not prescribe the same medication for different conditions, nor does it make sense to do the same exercise for different conditions. What's good for depression may actually make anxiety worse (you might be wondering "I have BOTH anxiety and depression. What do I do???" Don't worry my friend, I won't leave you hanging. We'll cover that in the chapter on "how to individualize"). What's good for one condition may not be good for another.

So who am I, and what qualifies me to write about exercise and nutrition for mental health?

I'm *Igor*. Hiya.

I have a degree in kinesiology and health science, as well as multiple diplomas in clinical nutrition. I was selected as one of the top 5 personal trainers in Toronto by the Metro News newspaper, written 4 other books besides this one, as well as over 400 articles (at the time of this writing) on my blog (FitnessSolutionsPlus.ca/blog). I've been hired by some of Canada's largest corporations to speak on the topic of mental health, and have done approximately 50 speaking engagements per year for the last 8 years.

But on a more practical level, the more I spoke about mental health, the more clients I got who had mental health issues. They didn't exercise for weight loss, toning or athletic purposes, like I was used to in the beginning of my career. No. They came because they wanted better mental health. Whether it was less anxiety, less depression, better mood, etc.

Of course, I pride myself on individualizing clients' exercise and nutrition programs, but I was never trained on how to modify a program when a person's main goal is improving mental health. My education involved learning how to train clients who want to lose body fat, get more toned, decrease back pain, recover from injuries and improve athletic performance. But not expressly on mental health. None of my personal training colleagues had any training on that, either, so I couldn't ask them.

No certifications or workshops existed on those topics, and no books had been written at that time. However, mental health was such a big issue that more and more companies started requesting that I speak on that topic, compared to my usual topic, which is *STOP EXERCISING! The Way You Are Doing it Now* (the title of my fourth book).

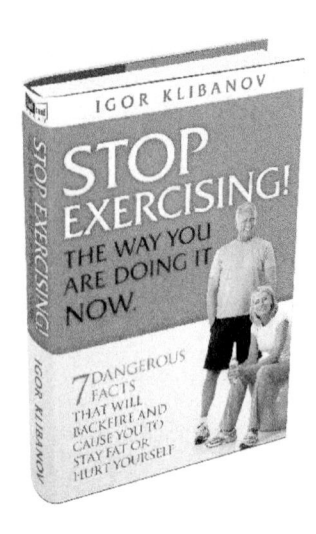

Exercise for mental health has remained largely an unexplored territory, so I had to do the research myself – on the exact exercise prescription for those conditions. And what you are reading about in this book is the compilation of years of research, and hundreds of studies perused.

But to bring the point home – the end results to the clients are often nothing short of life-changing.

As a result of using the right exercise and nutrition prescription, clients have:

- Reversed their conditions
- Improved their performance at work
- Been able to focus better

- Started new relationships that were personally satisfying

- Gotten off their medications (with their doctors' help)

- Lost weight

- Got more toned

- Had more energy

- Slept better

- Achieved mental clarity and a peace of mind

…and lots more.

And I hope this book brings the same benefits to you, the reader.

I've written the book to be as thorough as possible, but I know that with all the details, it can get overwhelming. That's why in the conclusion of this book, you'll find a quick reference guide. No theory, just practice. If you don't want to learn about the physiology behind mental health, and you're more of a "just tell me what to do" kind of person, just flip to the conclusion, and follow the recommendations in there. It will take you less than 5 minutes to get through that.

This page intentionally left blank

Exercise for Anxiety

If you have anxiety, you might feel that:

- You're constantly worrying, even though your life may be going well overall. You have a good job, good relationships, etc., but there's just this persistent sense of worry.
- You have a hard time falling asleep
- You might start "snapping" at people

Figure 1: **Signs of you may having anxiety**

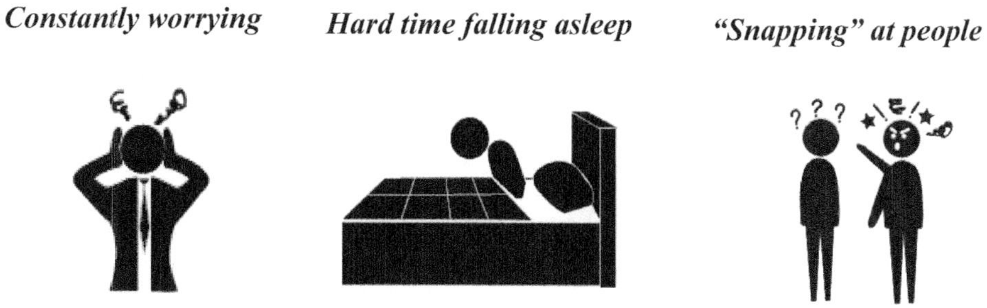

Constantly worrying   *Hard time falling asleep*   *"Snapping" at people*

I get it. Many of our clients have been there in the past. But fortunately, with the right combination of exercise, nutrition, and maybe psychotherapy and medications, you can start to feel better and better.

In this chapter, we'll focus strictly on how to **exercise for anxiety reduction**. We'll leave no stone unturned. We are going to answer questions like:

- What is anxiety? It seems like a silly question, but just so we're all on the same page, and we're working with the same definition, and so, we'll define it.

- What is the optimal exercise protocol for anxiety? What works better – cardio or strength training? How long do you need to exercise for? How soon can you see anxiety-reducing results?

- Do breathing exercises help reduce anxiety?

- How does exercise work to reduce anxiety? What are the mechanisms?

- What questions have yet to be answered? The whole field of "exercise as medicine" is still very new, the research is just in its infancy, and there is a lot more to be discovered about the subject

What is Anxiety?

What is it that differentiates plain old worry, from a clinical diagnosis of anxiety (or more accurately, **Generalized Anxiety Disorder**, or GAD)? According to the psychiatric diagnostic textbook, DSM-5, you have to meet certain criteria for a diagnosis of GAD. These criteria are:

1. Excessive worry that lasts **at least 6 months**. By "excessive", it is meant that the <u>worry is disproportionate to the actual risk</u>. Sometimes, this worry is generalized, and non-specific. There is no specific event causing worry. It's a diffuse sense of worry. You can't really pinpoint it as "if this problem were to go away, so would my worry."

2. It might be difficult to control the worry.

3. At least 3 of these symptoms must be experienced:

    - Edginess or restlessness

    - Feeling more tired than usual

    - Inability to concentrate

    - Irritability

    - Increased muscle soreness or pain

    - Difficulty sleeping (whether that's falling asleep, waking up throughout the night, or not feeling rested when you wake up)

    - Difficulty with daily functioning at work

Figure 2: **Generalized Anxiety Disorder explanation**

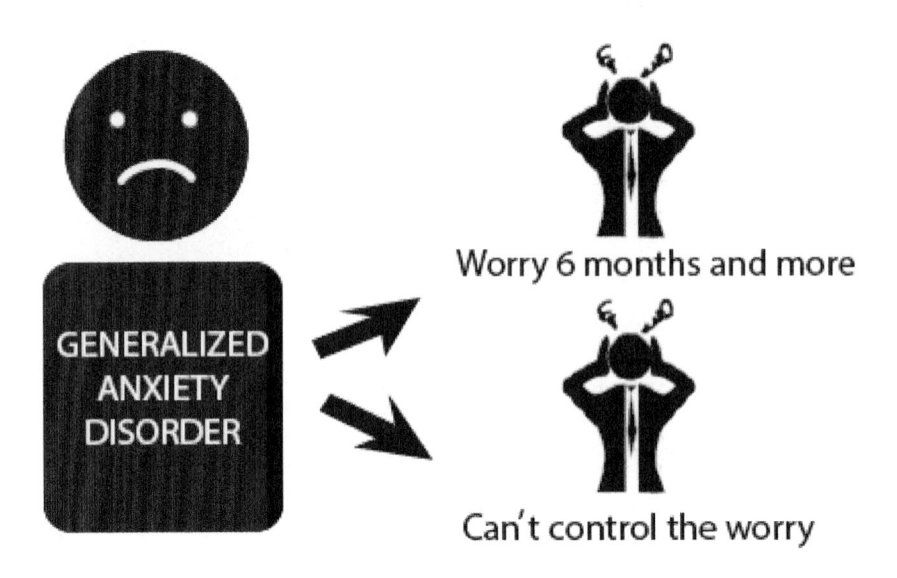

Worry 6 months and more

GENERALIZED ANXIETY DISORDER

Can't control the worry

Additionally, the anxiety cannot be related to:

- Other medical conditions
- Medications, drugs, or alcohol
- Another mental disorder

Figure 3: **Anxiety is not related to these situations**

Other medical conditions   *Medications, drugs or alcohol*   *Another mental disorder*

As you can see, there's a very precise definition of GAD. And since it's more of a cognitive disorder, it's not something you can look at blood and say "you have anxiety" in the same way that you can look at blood and say "you have high blood sugar." Therefore, GAD is really diagnosed and assessed with questionnaires. One of the most common questionnaires used for the assessment of anxiety is the **State-Trait Anxiety Inventory** (STAI).

Psychology
Clinical Psychology

State Trait Anxiety Inventory for Adults (STAI)

So now that we're all on the same page, and we have a standard definition of anxiety (I'll be using "anxiety" and "GAD" interchangeably throughout this chapter), let's start answering some of the most important questions about how to use exercise for anxiety reduction.

How to Exercise for Anxiety Reduction

Let me start this section off by saying that unfortunately, the research into what's optimal is not as robust as I'd like it to be, and there are still a lot of unanswered questions. But in this section, I'll summarize the available research on this topic.

Breathing, Yoga, Cardio or Strength Training?

Wouldn't it be awesome if there was just a single study that did a head-to-head comparison of these 4 types of exercise, to really determine what's best? Unfortunately, it doesn't exist, so we'll do the next best thing: look at the research that does exist.

In one study[1], researchers took 41 people with GAD, who have been on medications for at least 2 months, and for 4 weeks, the researchers asked them to do one 2-hour breathing training per week (under supervision), in addition to daily 20-minute breathing practices, on their own.

The result: after 4 weeks, **73% of people had a reduction in their anxiety, and 41% of people actually went into remission**.

Unfortunately, outside of that one study, I'm not aware of any others that either confirmed or refuted these results.

What about yoga? Yep, there's research on that as well (although not a lot).

In one study[2], researchers took 69 participants, all of whom had GAD, and they did 10 days of intense yoga, followed by daily yoga practice for 30 minutes, for 6 months.

The result: there was a **very large initial drop in anxiety**, followed by a plateau (but not a rise). So yoga also seems like a promising treatment for anxiety.

Figure 4: **The results of daily yoga practising for 6 months**

In one study[3], 42 participants who did not have GAD, but were nonetheless assessed on an anxiety questionnaire were divided into 4 groups:

- Group 1 had relatively low anxiety, and did cardio
- Group 2 had relatively low anxiety, and did strength training
- Group 3 had high anxiety, and did cardio
- Group 4 had high anxiety, and did strength training

What do you think the results were?

The study lasted for 16 weeks. None of the groups had any reductions in anxiety for the first 8 weeks. The anxiety reductions came during weeks 8 to 16. You can check out the results visually in the picture on the next page.

Both high-anxiety groups (groups 3 and 4) reduced their anxiety scores by a virtually equal amount (remember, anxiety is measured with the STAI questionnaire). The cardio group reduced it from 49.7 to 40.4. The strength training group reduced it from 47.6 to 38.5.

The low-anxiety group that did strength training (group 2), had no reductions in anxiety. But the low-anxiety group that did cardio (group 1) did have a small reduction in the anxiety score (from 29.9 to 26.8).

It would seem that **for people with a lot of anxiety, there's not much of a difference between strength training and cardio**. However, to complicate matters, one study has slightly conflicting results (as frequently happens in scientific research).

Figure 5: **Anxiety progress after 16 weeks, 4 different groups of exercising**

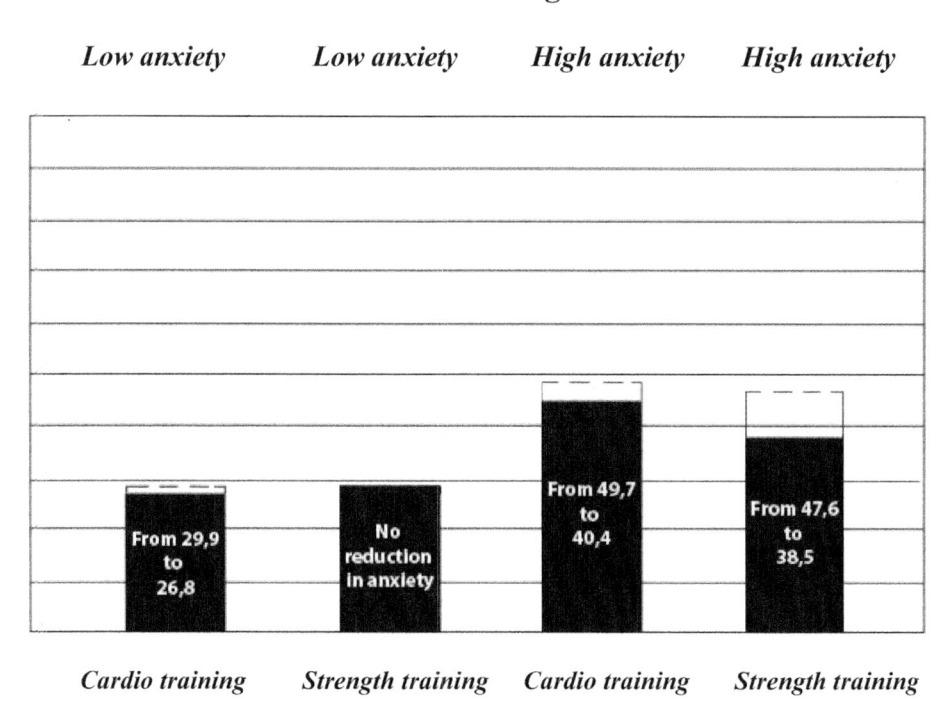

Low anxiety	*Low anxiety*	*High anxiety*	*High anxiety*
From 29,9 to 26,8	No reduction in anxiety	From 49,7 to 40,4	From 47,6 to 38,5
Cardio training	*Strength training*	*Cardio training*	*Strength training*

In one study[4], 30 women with GAD and on medications for their anxiety were divided into 3 groups:

- Group 1: strength training twice per week, lower body exercises only
- Group 2: cardio twice per week (cycling)
- Group 3: control group. They didn't exercise.

After 6 weeks, 30% of the people in the group that didn't exercise actually had a remission of their anxiety. Cool. I can just see the headlines now: "sit on your butt. Do nothing, and your anxiety will be relieved."

But wait a minute. There's more.

In group 2 (the cardio group), 40% experienced a remission of their anxiety.

In group 3 (the strength training group), 60% of experienced a remission of their anxiety.

So in this study, the clear winner was strength training. In the previous study, there was no clear winner.

Figure 6: **Results after 6 weeks training and medication of people with GAD, divided into 3 groups**

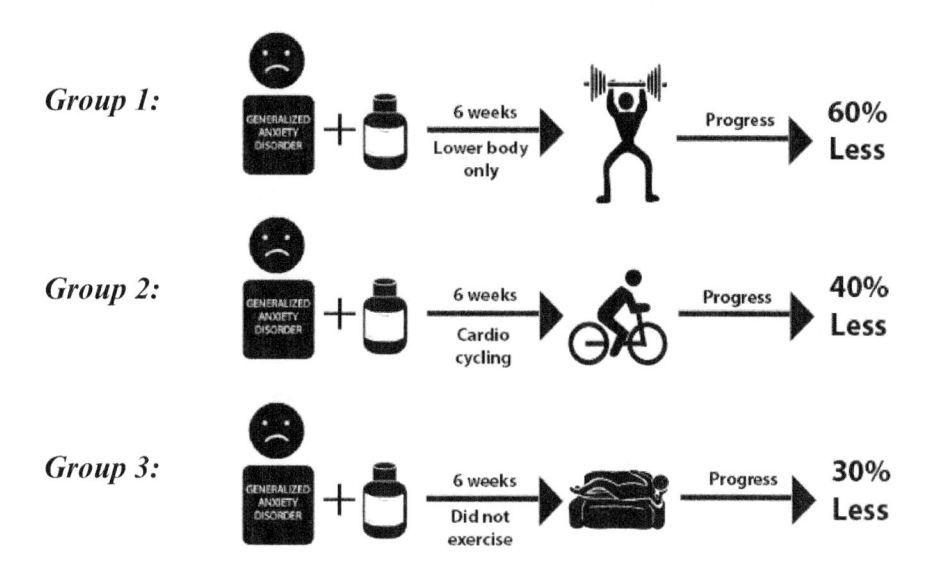

Group 1: GENERALIZED ANXIETY DISORDER + [medication] → 6 weeks Lower body only → Progress → **60% Less**

Group 2: GENERALIZED ANXIETY DISORDER + [medication] → 6 weeks Cardio cycling → Progress → **40% Less**

Group 3: GENERALIZED ANXIETY DISORDER + [medication] → 6 weeks Did not exercise → Progress → **30% Less**

One study[5] found reductions in anxiety immediately after strength training, but anxiety levels rose back to baseline as early as 20 minutes after exercise. However, another study[6] found that long-term strength training results in more stable reductions in anxiety (though unfortunately this study was not performed in people with GAD).

Sorry to confuse you with conflicting results. But towards the end of this chapter, I'll help you figure out what's best for you.

So we know that there's more than one way to "skin a cat." A lot of different forms of exercise help with anxiety. But what about intensity? What's the right intensity for anxiety relief? Fortunately, the research is much less conflicting on this issue.

One meta-analysis[7] (which is a study that analyzes many other studies) found that a single bout of **high-intensity strength training** (over about 70-85%) **either has no change, or increase in anxiety**. Whereas mostly **moderate intensity (50-60%) decreases anxiety**. In one study[8], participants even saw reductions in anxiety at 10% intensity. But there aren't any other studies that I'm aware of that attempted to answer the question of "what's the lowest intensity that will produce reductions in anxiety?"

Intensity in cardio is measured as a percentage of your maximal heart rate. A generally accepted formula for figuring out your maximal heart rate is 220 minus your age. So if you're 50, your maximal heart rate would be 170. Fifty percent of 170 would be 85 beats per minute. Sixty percent of 170 would be 102 beats per minute. So you would exercise in the 85-102 beats per minute range if you want to see reductions in anxiety. Keep in mind, that formula is not 100% accurate.

Intensity in strength training is measured in one of 2 ways. The first way is as a percentage of your 1 repetition maximum. In other words, it is the greatest amount of weight you can lift for one repetition. For anyone but a trained athlete, there's not much value, and too much risk in actually figuring out that number. That's why the second way might be safer. The second way to measure intensity in strength training is proximity to muscle failure. In other words, how many repetitions can you do, before you can no longer complete that exercise with proper technique? Let's say that number is 10 repetitions, and you want to work at an intensity of 50-60%, you would only do 5-6 reps, with a weight that if you were to push to the limit, you could do 10.

So now we know the intensity of exercise that's necessary to reduce anxiety, but what about duration? **How long do you need to exercise**? Most studies that show reductions in anxiety use exercise protocols that are in the 40-60 minute range, but that's more incidental. That's simply how long it takes participants to complete the amount of exercise.

But **what's the minimum required to reduce anxiety**? One study[9] looked at exercise durations of as little as 6 to 8 minutes, 5 times per week. Unfortunately, after 15 weeks of this, there were no reductions in anxiety. So 6 to 8 minutes is not enough.

However, in another study[10], people exercised for 20 minutes, 3 times per week, for 16 weeks, and in as little time as that, yes, anxiety was reduced.

In terms of the number of weeks required, there's no surprises there. One meta-analysis[11] found that exercise programs over 16 weeks have the greatest anxiety-reducing effects. Programs between

10 and 15 weeks have medium effects, and programs under 10 weeks have small effects.

And what about frequency? One meta-analysis[12] found that 3 to 4 days per week of exercise produces greater anxiety reductions than exercising less than 3 days per week or more than 4 days per week. This is an example of a case when "more is not better."

Now, we have a fairly precise idea of the type, intensity, duration and frequency to use when trying to exercise for anxiety reduction.

How Does Exercise Compare to Other Therapies?

One meta-analysis[13] that looked at 6 different studies noted that "Importantly, we have found a moderate effect (SMD =−0.58) on anxiety symptoms reductions, which is of similar magnitude of the anxiolytic effects from common pharmacotherapy such as paroxetine (SMD=−0.56), flouxetine (SMD=−0.56), quetiapine (SMD=−0.56), fluvoxamine (SMD=−0.60) and venlafaxine (SMD=−0.50) in people with anxiety disorders."

For people who aren't statistics geeks, SMD stands for "standard mean difference", which is the average difference in scores between 2 groups (for example, a group using medications, and a group not using medications.

This isn't an either/or type of scenario here, and it doesn't mean that you shouldn't use anti-anxiety medications. It simply means that you should be aware of the anxiety-reducing effects of both.

Why Does Exercise Work?

So we know that exercise works. Although there's debate about what works best, there's very little debate that it works. But the geeks among us (like me) want to take things one step further, and figure out <u>why</u> it works.

There are a number of theories on it. One theory about how exercise reduces anxiety is the distraction hypothesis[14]. Simply put, **if you're focusing on one thing, it provides a distraction from whatever is causing the anxiety**. If you're breathing hard from exercising, you focus on the workout, you temporarily forget about what's causing the anxiety.

Another theory is the serotonin hypothesis[15]. Serotonin is a neurotransmitter (brain chemical) that **makes you feel content and relaxed**. In people with anxiety, there is less serotonin in the brain, and exercise facilitates the production of serotonin.

Angela Clow and Sarah Edmunds, the authors of the book *Physical Activity and Mental Health* also propose a couple of other hypotheses.

For one, they propose that **exercise affects our brain waves**. There are 4 different kinds of brain waves that are produced based on what state you are in. Beta waves are the waves we normally produce when we are awake and alert. Alpha waves are the waves we normally produce when we are deeply relaxed. Like in those moments when you're lying in bed, and you're not quite asleep, but not quite awake, either. And then, there are delta and theta waves, which are produced during early sleep and during deep sleep, respectively. In people with anxiety, there aren't enough alpha waves, and exercise helps rebalance that.

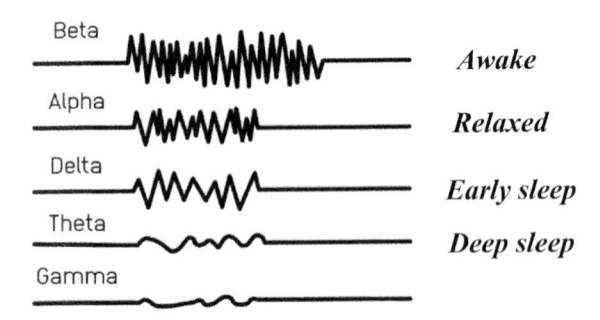

Figure 7: **Brain Waves**

Beta	*Awake*
Alpha	*Relaxed*
Delta	*Early sleep*
Theta	*Deep sleep*
Gamma	

Another theory by Clow and Edmunds is that **exercise raises the threshold at which anxiety is felt**. There's always some physical arousal, ranging from virtually none (as in deep relaxation or sleep), to a lot. In people with anxiety, the amount of physical arousal required for them to classify that as "anxiety" is lower than in people who don't have anxiety. Exercise helps raise that threshold.

As you can see, there are a number of ways that exercise for anxiety reduction works.

Unanswered Questions

As mentioned a number of times throughout this book, the whole field of "exercise as medicine" is still only in its infancy, and particularly with anxiety, there are still a lot of questions that the research hasn't yet gotten around to answering. Things that I would like to know are:

- What's the minimum "dose" of exercise required to have anxiety-reducing effects?
- What's the optimum "dose"?
- Is there a best "form" of exercise? Is cycling superior to swimming, vs. running, vs. aerobics classes, vs. lifting weights?
- Are there differences between men and women in how they respond to exercise? Does exercise reduce anxiety in one more than the other?

- Are there differences between the young and the elderly? Does exercise produce larger reductions in anxiety in one versus the other?

- Exercise isn't effective in everyone. How can we predict in whom exercise will not have anxiety-reducing effects? Which factors help determine this?

- What happens when you combine cardio and strength training? If you combine them, should you do both equally, or do cardio more than strength training, or otherwise? Do you get stronger anxiety-reducing effects? In theory, that might be the case, but in practice, it's not. Sometimes, the effects might be lower than either one by themselves, or they might be more than the expected combined value of each one. For example, it might be a 1 + 1 = 3 type of scenario.

… and lots of other questions.

What Works For You?

So you've just seen a bunch of studies on the topic of exercise and anxiety, but much of it is conflicting, and you might be more confused than clear. So let's end the confusion, and help you figure out what works <u>for you</u>, specifically.

Figure 8: **Different types of exercise can work for you**

GENERALIZED ANXIETY DISORDER

specifically

As I mention in my article on *the importance of measurements*[16], it's measuring your own results that helps you individualize, and tailor your approach. After all, what works for another person may not work for you.

As it pertains to anxiety, search online for an "anxiety questionnaire." Fill it out. Then start exercising on whatever kind of program you want. Strength training, cardio, yoga, anything. Do this 3-4 times per week, as per the guidelines from the research that we've covered here. Then, after one month, take the same questionnaire again. If your score improved, you know you found something that works (assuming no other changes in medication, diet, etc.). If your score didn't improve, try a different type of exercise, or exercise at a higher intensity, or lower intensity, etc.

Exercise Induced Panic Attack

How to Exercise When it Feels Like a Panic Attack

If you have anxiety, exercise is a double-edged sword. On the one hand, it has tremendous benefits, such as:

- Decreasing heart palpitations
- Sleeping better
- Reducing stress

Figure 9: **Exercise can help with anxiety**

Decreasing heart palpitations   *Sleeping better*   *Reducing stress*

But on the other hand, in some people with anxiety, **exercise can actually induce panic attacks**. Not just a little nervousness, but a full-blown panic attack, which may encompass:

- Shortness of breath
- Heart palpitations

- Nausea
- Dizziness
- Choking feeling
- Chest pain
- Thinking that you're having a heart attack, or that you're about to die.

So if you, or someone you know has anxiety, and gets this reaction from exercising, how does one get the upsides of exercise, without having to deal with any of the downsides? That's what we'll cover later in this book.

But first...

Why Can Exercise Induce A Panic Attack?

There are a lot of commonalities between exercise and a panic attack, like:

- Increased heart rate
- Increased adrenaline
- Faster respiratory rate (you breathe faster)
- Sweating

Figure 10: **There are a lot of commonalities between exercise and a panic attack**

Increased heart rate   *Increased adrenaline*   *Faster respiratory rate*   *Sweating*

If you have anxiety, and you've experienced a panic attack before, exercise can sometimes feel just like that. And it can be hard to tell the two apart. Once you reach a certain intensity threshold with your exercise, a panic attack comes immediately.

Strategies to Reduce Exercise-Induced Panic Attacks

Strategy #1: Proper Warm-Up and Cool-Down

Yes, this is a "basic" of exercise, but for someone suffering from exercise-induced panic attacks, this becomes that much more important.

If your normal heart rate is 70 beats per minute, and you just start exercising, withoumt a warmup, it can spike very quickly. It might go from 70 all the way to 150 in a matter of just a few seconds. To someone who doesn't suffer from panic attacks, that's not a big deal.

To someone who does suffer from panic attacks, this very sudden rise in heart rate might trigger a panic attack.

Figure 11: **Proper Warm – Up before exercise is basic**

To avoid triggering a panic attack, you want to gradually, and slowly increase your heart rate over a period of 5 to 10 minutes.

Likewise with a cool-down. Sometimes, panic attacks happen not during workouts, but after workouts. This can often be due to a sudden drop in heart rate. Again, that's something that can be avoided with a proper cool-down. Which, like a proper warm-up lasts 5 to 10 minutes.

Self-Reflection

After you experience a panic attack, it's important to **do a little introspection**. Although a panic attack is scary, it's not fatal, even though it feels like it at the time. So how can you take the edge off from panic attacks?

The next time you have a panic attack, reflect on it afterwards, and ask yourself two questions:

1. Did I die? This is a serious question.

2. Did it actually hurt?

This works better, if you **write down these questions, and the answers** to them using pencil and paper, as opposed to just verbalizing it.

You'll notice the answer to both questions is "no." It might not have been a comfortable experience, but it usually doesn't physically hurt. Do this after enough panic attacks, and eventually, the panic attacks decrease in intensity. If initially, you believed that you would die during a panic attack, the next time you have one, you'll remember that last time it happened, you didn't die. Knowing that you didn't die, and that you weren't hurt will make the next panic attack more tolerable. It still won't exactly be pleasant, but at least, you'll be less panicked, and better able to cope with it when it happens.

Exercise in a Comfortable Environment

You hear that exercise is good for anxiety, so you decide to join a gym that feels intimidating. There are people who look like they know what they are doing, and you are a first-timer, and you feel like everyone is watching you, and judging you.

Figure 12: **90% of time people will NOT judge you in a gym**

First of all, that's not true. For one thing, people are too self-conscious to worry about anyone else, but themselves (yes, even the ones that look like they're in really good shape). Others are too narcissistic, so they spend 95% of their gym time checking themselves out in the mirror. You have nothing to worry about.

But even so, it can be intimidating. So you have a couple of options:

1. Find a gym that isn't intimidating to you. Look for one where the people don't seem intimidating. Alternately, go to the gym when there aren't that many people around.

2. Work with a personal trainer who you're comfortable with, and makes you feel at ease.

Distract Yourself

Figure 13: **Find a way to distract yourself**

Sometimes, if you focus on the sensations you have during exercise, you'll notice that your heart rate speeds up, your breathing speeds up, you start to sweat, and that all reminds you of how you feel during a panic attack. So you start to backwards rationalize that you must be having a panic attack.

However, if there's a very engaging TV show that you're watching, it can make you forget that you're exercising and, it might just be the distraction you need.

Baby Steps

Start with an amount of exercise, that even you think is too low. You know how "they" say you need to exercise for ___ minutes (fill that in with whatever number you want… 30, 40, 60, whatever), or it doesn't count? Forget about that.

A 5-minute workout is better than a 0-minute workout. So do something light, and do something short. Right now, your goal is just to break the psychological connection between exercise and anxiety. **It takes a lot less time to break that connection, than it does to improve your cardiovascular fitness or your strength**.

Exercise for Depression

If you or someone you know is suffering from depression, you might notice that you:

- Have lost pleasure in activities that you really used to enjoy
- Aren't taking care of yourself as much
- Are neglecting certain relationships
- Performing worse at your work than you used to

Figure 14: **Signs you may be suffering from depression**

Have lost pleasure in many activities

Performing worse at work

Dont take care of yourself as muc

You are neglecting certain relationships

Then this chapter is for you.

What Is Depression?

What's the difference between general sadness, or a person randomly saying "I'm depressed", and a true, clinical diagnosis of depression (or the proper term - "Major Depressive Disorder")? For that distinction, we turn to the DSM 5, which is the Diagnostic and Statistical Manual of Mental Disorders, the "bible" that psychiatrists use for diagnosis.

So according to the DSM 5, for a person to be diagnosed with depression, he or she must:

- Have no other medical conditions, or drugs to which the depression can be attributed
- Suffer from some kind of occupational or social impairment
- Not have any other mental health issue
- Have not had any manic episode or hypomanic episode
- Have at least 5 of these symptoms:
  - Depressed most of the day, every day

- Decreased pleasure in activities that used to bring pleasure
- Weight loss or weight gain without trying
- Insomnia or hypersomnia
- Feeling "slowed down"
- Low energy levels
- Feelings of worthlessness or irrational guilt
- Unable to think clearly
- Thoughts of death/dying or suicidal thoughts

So now that we're all on the same page with the definition of depression, let's examine how to use exercise to reduce the symptoms of depression.

Type of Exercise for Depression: Cardio or Strength Training?

Although the occasional study finds that cardio is more effective, most studies[17] find **no difference in effectiveness between cardio and strength training**.

In one study[18], researchers divided participants into 2 groups:

Group 1 did cardio, 3 times per week, for 1 hour, at an intensity of 80% of their maximal heart rate (maximal heart rate is 220 minus your age. So if you're 50 years old, your maximal heart rate is in theory 170 beats per minute. 80% of that is 136 beats per minute)

Group 2 did strength training, 3 times per week for 1 hour. They did 10 exercises, in a circuit format, making sure their heart rate did not rise above 50-60% of their estimated maximum.

Group 3: control group. They didn't exercise.

And yes, both groups 1 and 2 had similar reductions in depression. After the study, **around 80% of the people in groups 1 and 2 no longer met the diagnostic criteria for depression**. But only 17% of the people in group 3 no longer met the diagnostic criteria for depression. Not bad, eh?

Figure 15: **There is no difference in effectiveness between cardio and strength training**

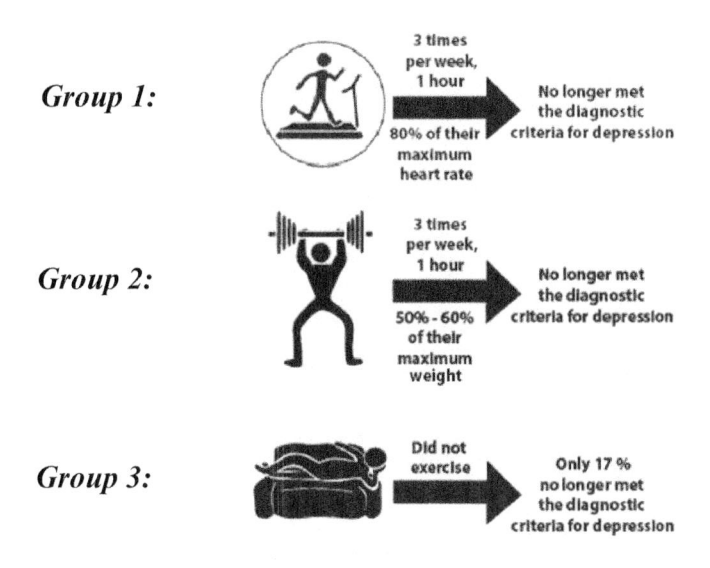

Group 1: — 3 times per week, 1 hour, 80% of their maximum heart rate → No longer met the diagnostic criteria for depression

Group 2: — 3 times per week, 1 hour, 50% - 60% of their maximum weight → No longer met the diagnostic criteria for depression

Group 3: — Did not exercise → Only 17 % no longer met the diagnostic criteria for depression

In another study[19], participants with depression, whose average age was 71 participated in high-intensity strength training, and after 10 weeks, those who were in the exercise group had a 54% reduction in their depression.

How Frequently Should You Exercise for Depression Relief?

That is, how many days per week? Is 1 day enough? Is 3 better? Is 5 better? Or is it like medications, where if you don't take it for one day, the effect completely goes away, in which case, you need to take it every day, 7 days a week?

That's what one study[20] tried to answer. In this study, researchers divided participants into 5 groups (this is about to get confusing, so if you want to see a picture of this, flip forward 2 pages):

- Group 1: control group (stretching)
- Group 2: burned 7 kcal/kg/week, across 3 days
- Group 3: burned 7 kcal/kg/week, across 5 days
- Group 4: burned 17.5 kcal/kg/week, across 3 days
- Group 5: burned 17.5 kcal/kg/week, across 5 days

If you're wondering what 7 or 17.5 kcal/kg/week means, it's referring to **calories burned**. So if you're an average person of 70 kg (154 pounds), at 7 kcal/kg/week, you're burning only 490 calories per week. If you're exercising 3 times per week (as in group 2), that's only 163 calories per workout. That's equivalent to maybe a 25-30 minute walk at a fast pace, or a 12-15 minute run.

If you're exercising 5 times per week (as in group 3), that's only 100 calories per workout.

At 17.5 kcal/kg/week, you're burning 1225 calories per week. Spread across 3 workouts, that's about 410 calories. Across 5 workouts, that's nearly 250 calories.

In this case, there was no difference between the 2 groups that burned 7 kcal/kg/week, and the group that didn't exercise at all. **None of those 3 groups saw much of a reduction in depression.**

However, both of the groups that exercised at 17.5 kcal/kg/week saw reductions in depression that were similar to each other.

And what were the reductions, exactly?

After 12 weeks of following this program, the reduction in depression symptoms was about 47%.

So what's our conclusion about frequency? From this preliminary evidence, it seems like there's **not much of a difference between 3 times per week, and 5 times per week, as long as you cross a certain energy expenditure threshold**. Is there a greater effect for even greater calorie expenditures? Maybe. But as far as I know, that research has not yet been done, so right now, it's an "I don't know."

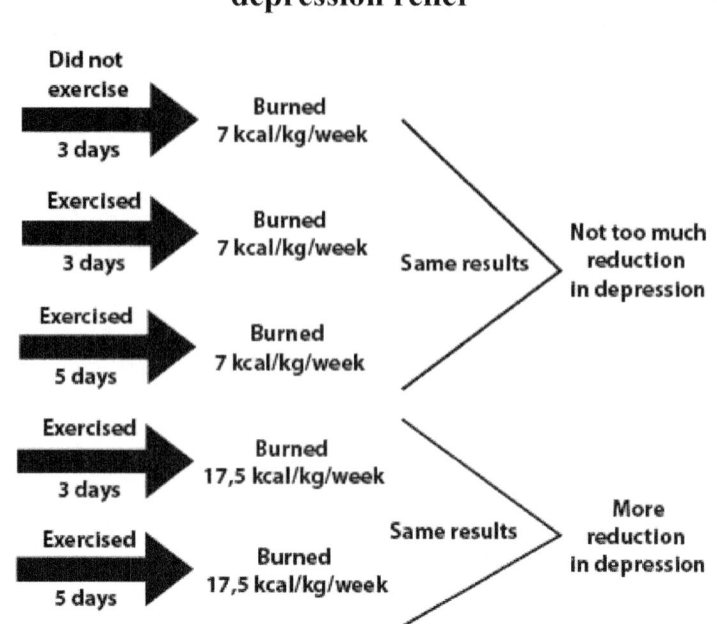

Figure 16: How frequently should you exercise for depression relief

- Did not exercise 3 days → Burned 7 kcal/kg/week
- Exercised 3 days → Burned 7 kcal/kg/week
- Exercised 5 days → Burned 7 kcal/kg/week

Same results → Not too much reduction in depression

- Exercised 3 days → Burned 17,5 kcal/kg/week
- Exercised 5 days → Burned 17,5 kcal/kg/week

Same results → More reduction in depression

Intensity of Exercise for Depression Reduction

Now, we know the type of exercise (cardio and strength training are about even), and the frequency of exercise (not much of a difference between 3 and 5 times per week). Now we want to know what's the intensity required to reduce depression? Should you take it easy? Or should you really push yourself?

That's what this study[21] tried to find out.

In that study, researchers divided participants into 3 groups:

Group 1 was a control group (they didn't exercise)

Group 2 did strength training at 80% of their maximum weight, 3 times per week for 8 weeks.

Group 3 did the exact same exercises, repetitions, and frequency as group 2, but they did it with only 20% of their maximum weight.

The results:

- 21% of the people in group 1 had a reduction in their depression after 8 weeks. Without exercise. Without medication. Without psychotherapy. It just happened.

- 61% of the people in group 2 had a reduction in their depression after 8 weeks.

- 28% of the people in group 3 had a reduction in their depression after 8 weeks

So what's our conclusion? **High intensity is superior to low intensity when it comes to depression reduction**.

Figure 17: **High intensity is superior to low intensity when it comes to depression reduction**.

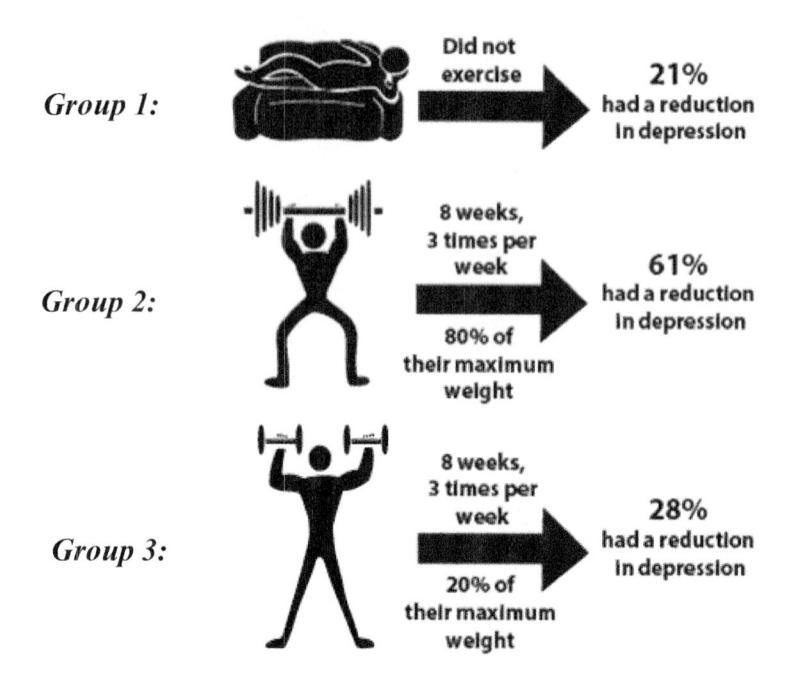

Group 1: Did not exercise → 21% had a reduction in depression

Group 2: 8 weeks, 3 times per week, 80% of their maximum weight → 61% had a reduction in depression

Group 3: 8 weeks, 3 times per week, 20% of their maximum weight → 28% had a reduction in depression

And yes, this study looked at strength training, but other studies[22] saw the same effect for cardio – **high intensity is required to reduce depression**. Why, you ask? Because you need to cross a certain intensity threshold before pain blocking chemicals are released. They're called "endorphins." Endorphins block physical pain, but there's a component of emotional pain that is felt in the same part of the brain, so endorphins help with that as well.

What about strength training intensity? It also needs to be high. In this study[23], researchers compared strength training at 80% of participants' maximal weight against the control group (who didn't exercise). The participants had an average age of 71, and for 10 weeks, they did traditional strength training exercises, 3 times per week, for 3 sets of 8 reps, at 80% of their maximal weight. Each session, the weight was increased as tolerated.

The results: the people in the group that were depressed reduced depression scores by 54%. The people in the control group (who didn't exercise, but did receive health education in a lecture style) reduced their depression score by only 22%.

So with depression, it's fairly conclusive that high intensity is necessary to reduce depression. How high is high? Over about 75% of your maximum.

How Long Do You Need to Exercise for Depression Relief?

Is this a case of "more is better", or is this a case of "just right"? Unfortunately, this variable hasn't been as well studied as frequency, intensity and type. However, one preliminary study[24] concluded that **duration is much less important than frequency and intensity**.

In terms of weeks/months, although small, transient reactions are seen with just a single exercise session, to see large, consistent, long-term reductions, you should exercise for **at least 9 weeks**[25].

Although I think that there should be no "end-point" to exercise – it's a lifestyle :)

Figure 18: **You should exercise for at least 9 weeks for results**

Exercise vs. Medications

And now, the million-dollar question: how do medications compare to exercise when it comes to depression relief?

One meta-analysis[26] (a study of several studies), from the journal Frontiers in Pharmacology looked at this question in very significant detail, and found that **exercise is equally effective to medications in the treatment of depression**. And when the two are combined, the medications work even better.

And yes, exercise has a few bonuses besides depression relief, like:

- Greater endurance
- Greater strength

- Greater flexibility
- Looking better
- Better self esteem
- Improved social life
- Improved relationships
- Better concentration
- Better performance at work

...the same can't be said for medications. That's not to say that they shouldn't be used, but in the risk/reward scale, exercise appears to be superior. It is much lower risk, but with the same reward.

The only difference is that it can be difficult to get a depressed person to start exercising, but it is much easier to get them to take a pill. As a result, smart doctors are getting their patients started with the medication, and once there's some relief, exercise is recommended on top of that.

Adherence to Exercise

Some of you might be thinking "well, that's nice and all, to know how to exercise if you have depression. But **how do I get a depressed person to exercise in the first place?**"

It's actually not that hard, and the adherence may not be as low as you think. Most studies[27] find that even in people with depression, **adherence to exercise is about 60 to 80%**.

But let's go back to our question - how can you get a depressed person into a regular exercise routine? There's a few ways that I can think of, from least to most effective.

Least effective (but still better than just telling them to exercise): **do less than you think you can**. If you think you can only do a 20 minute walk, go for a 15 minute walk. Make it easy. Get early successes, to get positive momentum going. At this point, the very beginning, it's more important to be consistent than to be optimal. As you become consistent, and you're in a regular routine, increase intensity and duration, until you get into what the research shows to be "optimal."

More effective: get an **accountability partner**. Have someone that you commit to exercising with. If you're on your own, you'll let yourself off the hook. If you're with an accountability partner, you're not just letting yourself down; you're letting them down. And you wouldn't want that; would you? :) An accountability partner can be a friend, a parent, a child, or heck, even a babysitter.

Most effective: **personal trainer.** Come on, you had to know I'd mention this. Obviously, I'm very biased. But it has all the benefits of an accountability partner, and takes it to the next level. An accountability partner is simply someone who you'll be accountable to. They take care of the consistency side of things, but not necessarily the effectiveness side of things.

Figure 19: **Ways to get depressed person to exercise**

Do less than you think you can   Accountability partner   Personal trainer

Your accountability partner may or may not be knowledgeable in proper exercise. And most likely, they are not knowledgeable in proper exercise for depression. Unfortunately, most personal trainers aren't either. However, the personal trainers who work with my company, are knowledgeable in that area. If you like this option best, might I say "Good choice." If you do want to work with us, fill out the application form on the website https://www.FitnessSolutionsPlus.ca, or email me at Igor@TorontoFitnessOnline.com.

What should you look for in a fitness facility when joining? Here are a few things just to get you started:

1. The people. Are they friendly and supportive, or are they unfriendly and intimidating (keep in mind, just because they're muscular doesn't mean they're unfriendly)
2. The environment. Is it clean, tidy, and well-maintained?
3. The circulation. Do you sense any stale air, or body odour?
4. Windows, so you can see outdoors.

And heck, despite those criteria, you might have selected the wrong gym, so don't sign up for a full year up front. Try just one month, or a 3-day pass (which a lot of gyms offer for free). If you like it, get a long-term membership. If you don't, try a different facility.

What about a personal trainer? What are some criteria to look for? Because the quality among trainers varies so widely, it's very important to pick a good one. Here are some criteria for that:

1. Does an initial assessment, and does assessments that are **relevant to you**. If you want better mental health, the trainer better do an assessment relevant to that goal.
2. Takes regular measurements of whatever variables are important to you. Whether it's body fat, mental health (ideally using some kind of questionnaire), etc.

3. Has a written program for you, not one made up on the spot.

4. Gives nutritional guidance.

5. Tracks your workouts, to make sure progress is being made

6. Is a fun and positive person to be around

Exercise for PTSD

While there's significantly less research on exercise for posttraumatic stress disorder (PTSD), it still has promise in improving symptoms, and in this chapter, that's what we will review.

We know a lot about the benefits of exercise, like:

- Improving strength
- Improving muscle mass
- Improving endurance
- Better body composition
- Greater energy

…and more.

But can exercise actually improve the symptoms of PTSD? Fortunately, the answer is "yes."

In one study[28], 81 participants with PTSD were divided into 2 groups:

- Group 1: standard treatment (psychotherapy, medications, and group therapy)

- Group 2: same as group 1 + exercise. Their exercise consisted of three 30-minute strength training sessions per week, plus walking.

After 12 weeks, group 2 had improved PTSD symptoms compared to group 1. What are those symptoms? Some of them are:

- Memories, thoughts and recollection of mental images from past stressful experiences
- Dreams of past stressful experiences, or variations of them
- Loss of pleasure in activities usually enjoyed
- Physical reactions (heart pounding, fast breathing, choking up, sweating, etc.) to memories of a stressful event.

Figure 20: **Exercise can improve symptoms of PTSD**

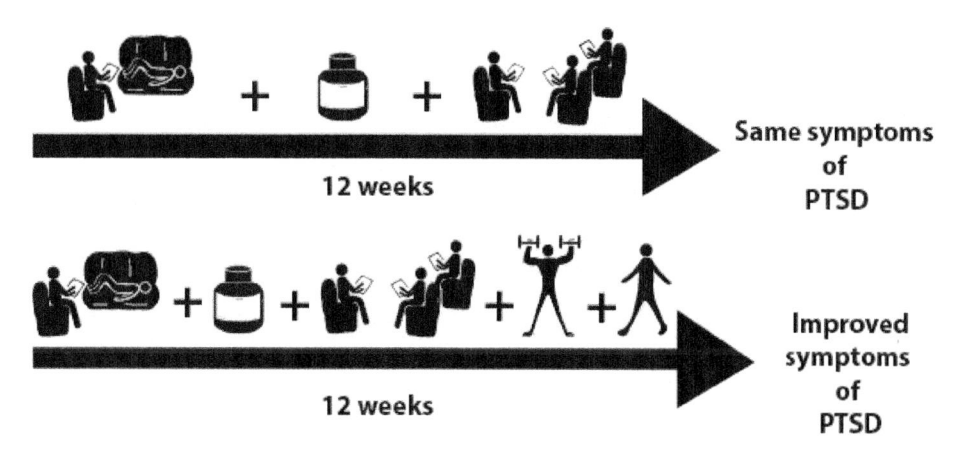

The entirety of the symptoms can be looked up by simply searching "PCL-C" on the internet.

Although this study was based around strength training, another one[29] showed the effectiveness of cardio for PTSD. For 12 weeks, 16 women did cardio 3 times per week for 30-40 minutes. After that period of time, their symptoms of PTSD improved significantly.

And one other study[30] showed that even stretching and deep-breathing exercises improved symptoms of PTSD.

Unfortunately not enough research exists yet about exercise for PTSD as there is for anxiety and depression, where specific recommendations can be made for type (cardio vs. strength training vs. stretching), frequency, intensity, and duration.

There are still questions about exercise for PTSD that need to be answered, such as:

- What's the minimum amount of exercise that needs to be done to see reductions in PTSD symptoms? Can someone exercise once per week and still see improvements?

- Is it a dose-response type of relationship, where more exercise is better, or is it a "diminishing returns" type of relationship - where you reach a certain point that if you go above that point, there are no more additional improvements, or possibly, even detriments?

- What about supervised exercise (like with a personal trainer or researcher), versus unsupervised exercise? Is there a difference in effectiveness?

...and others.

However, from the research that does exist, a few recommendations can be made:

- It seems like all 3 major types of exercise are effective – strength training, stretching, and cardio
- Durations need to be about 30 minutes or more
- Frequency needs to be 3 times per week or more

How to Individualize (Questionnaire)

The last few chapters, you've been reading "this type of exercise is good for this, but this type of exercise is good for that." And you might be thinking "I have several mental health diagnoses. What do *I* do?"

Fortunately, the practice is much easier than the theory.

You've read that high intensity is better for depression, but moderate intensity is better for anxiety. Or that cardio is better for one, but strength training is better for another.

So where do you start?

With an assessment. As I'm fond of saying in my seminars, and in my articles, "If you're not assessing, you are guessing."

So let's assess the impact of different forms of exercise on your mental health.

How do you do that? With our clients, we use a super-simple 5-symptom questionnaire.

Rate these feelings on a 0-5 scale as you're feeling right before a workout (0: I don't feel this at all; 5: I feel this very intensely):

Anger: 0 1 2 3 4 5

Confusion: 0 1 2 3 4 5

Sadness: 0 1 2 3 4 5

Vigor: 0 1 2 3 4 5

Fatigue: 0 1 2 3 4 5

And then repeat this questionnaire immediately after the workout, before you even leave the facility, to go home.

The key with this questionnaire, however, is to test different workouts. Here are some examples:

- Cardio, steady pace
- Cardio, intervals
- Strength training, high reps/low weight (high reps is over 15)
- Strength training, moderate reps/moderate weight (moderate reps is 8-12)
- Strength training, low reps/high weight (low reps is 7 or less)
- Yoga
- Fitness classes (Zumba, Aquafit, etc.)
- Rock climbing

- Dancing
- Whatever else appeals to you

So test several different kinds of workouts, and see what has the largest impact on this short, but effective questionnaire.

And stick with the workout that has the largest positive effect.

If you find that multiple workouts have very similar positive effects, you can rotate through them. So for example, if you found that you had great improvements in mood in response to yoga, rock climbing, and interval training, do those.

If you have a workout partner, or personal trainer, it may be worthwhile to test the effect of the workout with a trainer/partner versus without them. A few things can happen:

- When doing the workout on your own, you get small elevations in mood, but when doing it with a partner/trainer, you get large elevations in mood. This would tell you that your mental health condition is partially due to physiology, and partially due to lack of positive social interactions.

- You get large elevations in mood by yourself, but decreases in mood with a partner/trainer. This may be the case if you don't like the person, or you're more of an introvert, and like your quiet time.

- You see no differences in scores between working out by yourself versus with a trainer/partner.

Also, keep in mind that different partners/trainers may have different impacts on your mood when exercising.

For instance, if your partner whines and complains a lot, he or she may not be the right partner for you. Likewise, if a trainer is pushing you to do things you are not comfortable doing, that person may not be the right trainer for you. It's important to find someone who makes the program fit to you. Not to make you fit to the program. A good trainer should make exercise client-centred, not program-centred.

Mechanisms: Why Exercise Improves Mental Health

Reason #1: **Endorphins**

When you exercise at a high intensity, it's physically uncomfortable. You're out of breath, and your muscles are burning. Your body doesn't like that, so it releases "pain-blocking" chemicals called "endorphins." It makes sense why high intensity workouts are required for depression reduction. It has to be uncomfortable enough to trigger the release of endorphins. **Low intensity is too comfortable for endorphin release**.

And yes, it blocks physical pain, but along with that, it apparently helps emotional pain, as seen in depression.

Reason #2: **Self Efficacy Hypothesis**

Often, a person who suffers from depression has the feeling like their life is out of control. Things are happening to them, and they are helpless against circumstances. **Exercise gives you a sense of control**. You know that if you go for an intense 20-minute workout, you'll feel better. And who controls when you work out? You do! Who controls how long you work out? You do! Who controls how hard you work out? You do! So you re-gain the sense of control.

Reason #3: **Distraction**

Sometimes, exercise just works because you're focused on how hard you're breathing, and how much your muscles are burning. You just forget whatever is causing your mental health issues.

Reason #4: **Sleep Improvement**

It's very well-known that **people who exercise sleep better.** And people who sleep better have better mood. So this is yet another mechanism. Often people with anxiety, depression, PTSD and other mental health issues have poor sleep as a contributing cause.

Reason #5: **Serotonin**

Serotonin is the "happy chemical", and when it's released, you feel content and relaxed. Guess what helps increase serotonin in the brain? Yep, it's exercise.

Reason #6: **Brain Waves**

Angela Clow and Sarah Edmunds, the authors of the book *Physical Activity and Mental Health* also propose a couple of other hypotheses.

For one, they propose that **exercise affects our brain waves**. There are 4 different kinds of brain waves that are produced based on what state you are in. Beta waves are the waves we normally produce when we are awake and alert. Alpha waves are the waves we normally produce when we are deeply relaxed. Like in those moments when you're lying in bed, and you're not quite asleep, but not quite awake, either. And then, there are delta and theta waves, which are during early sleep and during deep sleep, respectively. In people with anxiety, there aren't enough alpha waves, and exercise helps with that.

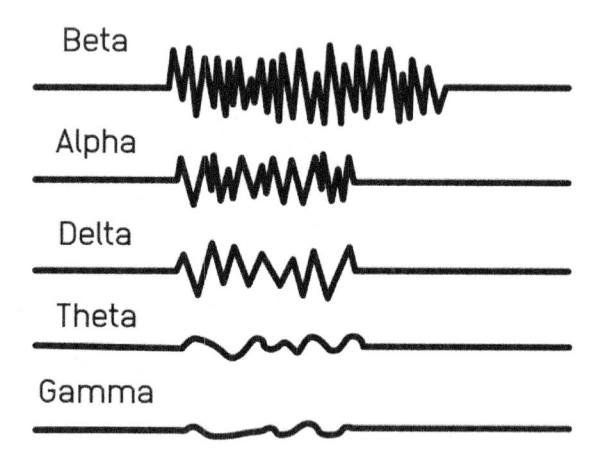

Reason #7: **Anxiety Threshold**

There's always some physical arousal, ranging from virtually none (as in deep relaxation or sleep), to a lot. In people with anxiety, the amount of physical arousal required for them to classify that as "anxiety" is lower than in people who don't have anxiety.

The "stress hormone" is called "cortisol", and we have some of it in our blood at all given times. However, two people may have the exact same blood level of cortisol, yet the one without anxiety classifies that as "generalized arousal" or excitement. The one with anxiety classifies that level of cortisol as anxiety.

Exercise helps this person with anxiety raise the threshold at which they feel anxious.

Nutrition for Anxiety

In my seminars, I often joke that nutrition for mental health is simple: all you need is chocolate and red wine. And I get a lot of laughs.

Unfortunately, it's not quite as simple as that. Fortunately, just as there is a lot of opportunity to improve mental health with exercise, there are certainly ways to improve mental health with nutrition as well.

In this chapter, we'll talk about:

- The 2 most common misdiagnoses of anxiety, and how to make sure your anxiety is really anxiety, and not something else

- How caffeine and aspartame can cause or contribute to anxiety

- How your digestive health can influence anxiety

Anxiety Misdiagnosis: Is it Your Thyroid?

A relatively common misdiagnosis of anxiety is hyperthyroidism (a fast thyroid). The thyroid is a butterfly-shaped gland that sits behind the windpipe, and it's like the gas pedal on your metabolism.

Figure 21: **Sometimes your thyroid is the reason you have anxiety**

When it's working properly, everything is hunky-dory:

- Good hair quality
- Good skin quality
- Great mental focus
- Good sleep
- Good bowel movements

...and so on.

When it's going too fast, life isn't so peachy. You get:

- Frequent bowel movements (know what I'm saying?)
- Too much sweating
- Weight loss (don't get too excited... it's both fat AND muscle)

...and, as it pertains to this chapter: **anxiety**.

So to ensure that your anxiety is truly anxiety, you need to have your thyroid checked. And the most common test for the thyroid is the TSH, but unfortunately it doesn't tell you the full picture.

Figure 22: Difference between properly working and fast working thyroid

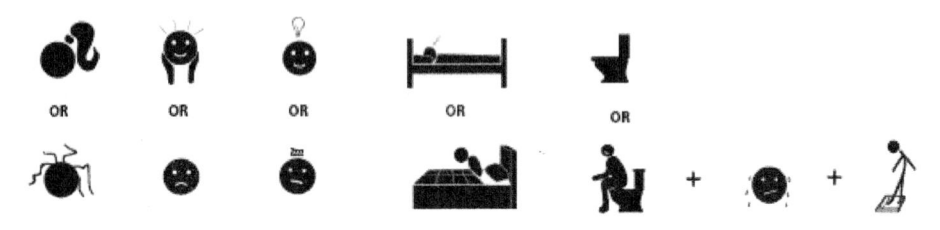

To get a complete picture of what's going on, you also want to run these tests:

- Free T3
- Free T4
- rT3 (that's reverse T3)
- TBG
- Anti-TPO antibodies
- Anti TGB antibodies (not to be confused with TBG)
- T3 Uptake

Of course, unless you know how to interpret these tests, the actual scores are meaningless, so make sure you work with someone skilled at interpretation.

So let's say that you do have hyperthyroidism, what do you do? While a complete outline of the "hyperthyroidism diet" is beyond the scope of this book, since that could be a book in and of itself, here are the bare bones:

- Eat a low-iodine diet. Which foods contain high amounts of iodine?
    - Iodized salt
    - Most fish (especially cod)
    - Algae
    - Kale
    - Seaweed
    - Dairy
- Eat foods that are high in selenium, like:
    - Brazil nuts (6-8 nuts will do. Too much can be dangerous as well)
    - Pork
    - Beef

- Turkey
- Eggs

Figure 23: **Foods with high amounts of iodine**

Algae and seaweed   Most fish   Iodized salt   Kale

Figure 24: **Foods with high amounts of selenium**

Pork   Beef   Turkey   Eggs

Another Common Misdiagnosis: Low Blood Sugar

Sometimes, low blood sugar (AKA hypoglycemia) may either be a contributing factor, or even the root cause of anxiety.

To understand why this happens, let's consider the physiology and the endocrinology of hypoglycemia.

Whenever you eat a meal that's rich in carbohydrates, blood sugar rises. When blood sugar rises, insulin rises shortly after to tell the cells (muscle cells, fat cells, liver cells, etc.) to "open up" their gates to let sugar out of the blood and into those cells. Once those cells receive the signal, they do what they're told, and blood sugar returns to normal.

That's a healthy, normal, desirable response. The problem happens when those cells do open up their "gates", and blood sugar drops too quickly.

However, just like in the Goldilocks tale, blood sugar shouldn't be too high, or too low. It should be just right. Generally speaking, "just right" is around 4.5-5.5 mmol/l. But if it goes too low, your body starts to see it as an emergency, and wants to get it back up to that optimal range immediately. How does it do that? By releasing 5 hormones that raise blood sugar: growth hormone, cortisol, glucagon, noradrenaline, and adrenaline. Whereas the first 3 hormones take some time to be released, the last 2 are released in a matter of seconds.

And as they're often called, noradrenaline and adrenaline are the "fight or flight" hormones. When they are released they give you a sense of urgency, and that can trigger anxiety symptoms.

How might you know if your anxiety is caused by low blood sugar? Here are a few clues:

- If your anxiety is worse right before meals
- If eating a meal relieves anxiety symptoms
- If you have a "crash" (increased anxiety), and eating sugar or something sweet relieves those symptoms

…then there's a strong possibility that your anxiety is either caused by, or at least made worse by low blood sugar.

Figure 25: **Symptoms anxiety is caused by low blood sugar**

Worse right before meals and eating relieves symptoms

Sugar relieves symptoms

What makes it challenging from a diagnostic perspective is that there's no agreement on exactly how low is "low blood sugar."

Some researchers recommend using 3.3 mmol/l (that's 60 mg/dl for my American readers). Other researchers recommend using 2.8 mmol/l (50 mg/dl). And yet other researchers recommend using a number that is 1 mmol/l below that specific person's fasting level. Last but not least, a fourth suggestion is if low blood sugar symptoms are experienced during an oral glucose tolerance test, even if blood sugar levels are normal (perhaps it's the speed with which blood sugar comes down, as opposed to the absolute level).

Regardless of how low blood sugar is defined, if it's suspected as a cause, the solution is simple, and harmless: stabilize blood sugar.

How do you do that?

- Eat 4-6 small, frequent meals throughout the day that contain both fat and protein (things like meat, fish or seafood, nuts and seeds, beans, etc.)

- Consume the majority of carbohydrates from low glycemic sources. "Low glycemic" means that they don't raise blood sugar quickly. For example, minimize rice, white potatoes, pasta, and bread, and instead, emphasize things like beans, quinoa, buckwheat, peas, lentils, sweet potatoes, etc.

- Avoid alcohol, because the sugar in alcohol is digested very quickly, and can cause a blood sugar crash

- Avoid refined sugar. This will often come with withdrawal symptoms, so expect those for a few days, up to a week. It will take approximately 2 weeks for the taste buds to readjust, and stop craving high levels of sugar.

Figure 26: **Ways you can stabilize blood sugar**

Eat well   *Avoid alcohol*   *Avoid refined sugar*

Additionally, certain supplements may help, like:

- Chromium: 200-1000 mcg/day, in divided doses
- L-Carnitine: 500-2000 mg/day
- B complex vitamins

Is your coffee addiction contributing to your anxiety?

The coffee addicts among the readers may recoil in denial that perhaps caffeine is contributing to their anxiety. But the research is strong on this one.

One study[31] in fact, is even titled "anxiety or caffeinism: a diagnostic dilemma." Which shows you that the symptoms of high caffeine consumption can be nearly indistinguishable from the symptoms of anxiety. And two other studies[32, 33] showed that the more you drink the worse your anxiety.

Figure 27: **Sometimes coffee can contribute your anxiety**

I know what you might be thinking: "but I know someone who drinks more coffee than me, but doesn't have anxiety. So it can't be that." Ah, I can feel the denial. You're right – not everyone has the same response to caffeine. However, those people who are predisposed to anxiety tend to be way more responsive to the effects of caffeine compared to those who are not predisposed to anxiety.

In one study[34] of people with anxiety who were hospitalized for 6 months, their caffeine intake was completely restricted for 3 weeks, and their anxiety improved significantly. After the 3 weeks, they resumed their regular caffeine consumption, and all their symptoms returned.

You might be wondering "why does caffeine contribute to anxiety?" There are multiple reasons:

1. It increases how long cortisol (the stress hormone) stays in the blood. As you'll recall from the chapter on exercise for anxiety, people with anxiety have a lower cortisol threshold before they classify that level of cortisol as "anxiety", and caffeine keeps it up.

2. It increases adrenaline, and in someone with anxiety, it doesn't take a large increase to trigger symptoms

3. It can make symptoms of low blood sugar worse, and low blood sugar can trigger anxiety for reasons we've talked about earlier in this chapter.

So what do you do? You run a self-test: for 4 weeks, eliminate caffeine completely, from all sources – coffee, tea, chocolate, etc. Note how your anxiety changes over this period of time. After 4 weeks, bring it back in, and see what happens. If your symptoms return, it's probably a good idea to keep it out permanently. If your symptoms don't return, you can continue consuming it.

And a word of warning: you probably already know this if you've tried to kick your caffeine habit in the past – there will be withdrawal symptoms. You'll get a bad headache, your energy will be low, and in severe cases, your vision may even get blurry. That's OK. It'll last for only a few days, and up to a week. Stay strong during this time, and expect it.

Aspartame

This one has weaker evidence behind it than caffeine, but nonetheless, it's something worth investigating if you have anxiety.

Aspartame is an artificial sweetener, and it's found in pop, gum, and most things that are "sugar-free" or "low sugar" (like ice cream, candy, etc.)

Although this doesn't happen in everyone, it seems that in people predisposed to anxiety, aspartame can decrease the release of certain neurotransmitters (brain chemicals) in the brain. Among those is serotonin (the happy chemical), dopamine (the reward chemical) and norepinephrine (the energy chemical).

Additionally, aspartame raises the levels of cortisol[35].

So it made sense mechanistically, and the case studies[36] back it up. In people who were being treated for anxiety, when they removed aspartame from their diet, their symptoms improved. When they started consuming aspartame again, either on purpose, or accidentally, their symptoms returned in a matter of hours to days.

I don't know about you, but if you have anxiety, this seems like a worthwhile attempt.

Is Your Digestion Causing Your Anxiety?

A very robust area of research that is quickly growing is in what's called the "gut-brain axis." That is, the digestive system "talks" to the brain, and the brain "talks" back.

Just think about common sayings in our culture:

- "I have a gut feeling"
- "Listen to your gut"
- "I have butterflies in my stomach"

It seems that we know intuitively that our gut can "think." And sure enough, research is backing this up.

Figure 28: **Gut feeling**

Old-time doctors (from ancient Greece and Rome) would often say "disease begins in the gut." And they were referring to most disease – not just gastrointestinal issues. They would talk about skin issues, heart issues, hormonal issues, and yes – psychiatric issues.

Finally, more and more research is emerging in this field, with terms like "microbiome" the "gut-brain axis", "leaky gut" and "intestinal permeability" entering the lexicon. And that research is very compelling.

So I know you must be thinking – "how does my digestive health influence my brain health?" Good question, my inquisitive reader. There are a few different ways in which this connection happens:

1. You know those "brain chemicals" (neurotransmitters) we talked about earlier, like serotonin, dopamine, and others? Well, they are used by the brain, but they are not necessarily made in the brain. They're made largely in the small and large intestines. As much as 70-90% of the serotonin (the "happy chemical") that we have is made in the small intestine. Not the brain.

2. The bacteria in our intestines (known as "flora" or "probiotics") are involved with hormone regulation[37]. They regulate hormones like insulin, glucagon, estrogen, and others. And we've already discussed, insulin and glucagon can impact blood sugar, which in turn will impact brain health.

3. According to one study[38], and others, we have a nerve that goes all the way from the brain to the digestive system, called the "vagus nerve." This nerve "senses" the mix of different bacteria that we have in our intestines. If this mix is off, then it will carry that information back up to the brain, and the brain responds correctly (producing anxiety or depression) to an incorrect stimulus.

These connections aren't purely theoretical, either.

In one study, mice were put on a high fat diet, so as to cause obesity, and the behaviours that indicated anxiety were observed. Sure enough, those behaviours increased as the mice gained weight. But the interesting part is two-fold:

1. When these now-overweight mice were given antibiotics, their behaviors associated with anxiety went away, without weight loss.

2. When bacteria from these overweight anxious mice were transferred into the intestines of sterile mice, these sterile mice developed symptoms of anxiety as well.

3. When bacteria from overweight mice who received antibiotics were transferred into the intestines of sterile mice, these sterile mice did not develop symptoms of anxiety.

Now granted, humans aren't mice, so you can't generalize, but this kind of research is not possible in humans (can you imagine feeding people until they got fat and developed anxiety, giving them antibiotics, and seeing what happens?)

However, even in humans, studies have shown differences in the bacteria living inside the intestines of people with mental health issues, vs. without them.[39]

So how might you know if your mental health issues are being caused by problems with your digestion? Here are a few clues:

- You have constipation
- You have diarrhea
- You've used antibiotics for a prolonged period of time
- You eat an unhealthy diet
- You have sugar cravings
- You have gas
- You experience bloating
- If your mental health issues were preceded by some kind of virus or bug, possibly while travelling

Figure 29: **Mental health issues can be caused by problems with your digestion**

Constipation   Unhealthy diet   Antibiotics   Having gas and bloating

The more of these you have, the higher the likelihood that your anxiety is at least partially (and possibly entirely) caused by digestive disturbances.

However, even if you don't have any digestive symptoms, it doesn't totally rule out the role of digestion in your anxiety.

Multiple studies have found that even in people with absolutely no digestive symptoms/complaints, removing gluten (therefore improving the balance of bacteria) improved mental health[40].

So if you may or may not have symptoms, how do you know whether your digestion is implicated in your mental health issues?

You can do a symptom questionnaire, and you can also run a comprehensive digestive stool analysis (CDSA), but you need a trained professional to interpret the results for you. This will give you a much clearer idea as to whether your digestion is playing a role in your mental health issues.

Now, let's say that you've found that your digestion is indeed playing a role. What do you do to "fix your gut?"

A common go-to is what's called the "4R program", popularized by Dr. Jeffrey Bland.

It breaks down like this:

- Remove – infections, allergies, sensitivities
- Replace what's missing. Typically, that's stomach acid and enzymes
- Reinoculate – bring back the healthy bacteria that should be in your intestines in the first place
- Repair – the digestive lining. The layer that coats the stomach, to protect the walls of the stomach from the stomach acid.

Since I wrote about this extensively in one of my other books, *STOP EXERCISING! The Way You Are Doing it Now,* with my permission, I'll just copy and paste it here (isn't it great when I don't have to ask anyone for permission to copy my own work?):

Remove

First, you have to figure out what food sensitivities are keeping the inflammation cycle in your gut since that is yet another stress on the body.

The difference between a food allergy and sensitivity is simply this: if you have an allergy, the reaction is severe and immediate. If you have a food sensitivity the reaction is subtle and delayed. Our goal is to eliminate both from your diet. Although people tend to automatically eliminate foods to which they are allergic because of the symptoms that occur, rarely do we pay attention to food sensitivities. This is because the effects of the foods ingested are subtle and delayed (by hours to days) so we often do not make the connection with the delayed symptoms.

Some of these symptoms include nasal congestion a few hours after eating or achy body the following day.

In order to investigate food sensitivities in my clients, I prefer to use a test that measures IgG, IgA, IgM and IgE which is a laboratory test that accurately pinpoints food sensitivities. This test lists approximately 200 different foods.

If you prefer to not do the lab test, then you can go the route of doing an elimination diet. The downside of this option, although it may cost a lot less, is that you have to exercise self-discipline. To accurately find out what you are sensitive to, you *have* to eliminate the most common allergens for the four-week test period.

This means reading labels and being very careful about what you eat. That leaves you with plenty of vegetables (except for potatoes, tomatoes, bell peppers, egg plants, corn, and chili peppers), most meats (except pork), and most nuts and seeds, in addition to all fruit. You can eat any of these in unlimited quantities. You should not go hungry -this is important.

If you have no time or patience for either option, eliminate the most common allergens in North America, which are gluten, dairy, sugar, corn, and soy. This is the least-preferred option out of the three because it is not specific to your body or its needs.

Replace

Replace that which was lost, such as digestive enzymes and restore stomach acid. Be sure to take high-quality digestive enzymes which help with the digestion of proteins, carbohydrates, and fats. These enzymes are protease, amylase, and lipase.

Reinoculate

Probiotics are friendly microorganisms that populate the small intestine, as we already discussed. You want to have more good bacteria in your gut than bad bacteria.

Most companies do not produce high-quality probiotics. Choose a capsule that has between 15 and 60-billion live bacteria in it.

Many think of yogurt as a good source of probiotics, but it contains an inadequate number to make much difference to your intestinal population. Choose a product that is guaranteed at the time of expiry, *not* at the date of manufacture and packaging, because some bacteria die off before you consume the capsules.

Different strains of bacteria have different lifespans. Companies who make high-quality probiotics compensate for the anticipated loss of bacteria in the time it takes the product to get to consumers. Additional bacteria are placed into the product to ensure a high number of bacteria survive to do their job in your intestines.

Check the product label for these very important words: "live and active cultures."

Additionally, eating foods that contain probiotics can be helpful. These foods include:

- Kefir
- Sauerkraut
- Yogurt
- Kimchi
- Kombucha

Prebiotics are the foods that probiotics eat! Feed those little guys what they need to survive and thrive. Prebiotics are found in bananas, honey, garlic, onions, and whole

grains. If a person is working on killing some bad bacteria and Candida, it's important to avoid fruits for a period of time (one to three weeks). So get your prebiotics through

supplements initially. Then you can switch to food sources.

Figure 30: **High – quality probiotics**

Bananas *Onion* *Yogurt* *Grains*

Repair

It is essential that the lining of your digestive system is healthy. If there has been any damage, healing and repair need to take place before proper digestion and health can be maintained. The stomach has a coating around it which prevents it from being worn-out by the highly acidic hydrochloric acid, which can burn through a car hood if poured onto a car.

Glutamine helps to repair stomach lining. In addition to glutamine you can use DGL (*Deglycerrized* licorice) and aloe vera to repair the digestive lining.

In conclusion, it is essential to improve and maintain your digestive health. In taking steps to do so, you will reap the benefits and your body will thank you for it.

The Inflammation Connection

We hear that word all the time – "inflammation." But what is it really? Inflammation is the immune system's response to a real or perceived threat. That response includes increased white blood cells (of which, there are many different subtypes), in order to identify and destroy the offending substance.

You might be thinking "inflammation is an issue of the immune system. What's the connection to a psychiatric condition, like anxiety?" I'll tell you.

One study[41] found inflammation to inhibit the parts of the brain called the "basal ganglia" and "cortical reward centre." These parts of the brain are responsible for motivation, learning, and a few other functions.

Sure enough, one study[42] found a strong connection between anxiety and inflammation (measured using a blood test called "CRP" or "C-Reactive Protein").

Now granted, correlation does not equal causation, but nonetheless, it's worth addressing inflammation in its own right.

What are the basics of reducing inflammation?

- Identify if there are any viruses, parasites, bacteria or fungi present in your body, which shouldn't be there. You'll need the help of a doctor for this. A basic complete blood count that looks at your white blood cells will give you a clue. A CDSA will give you even more precise results.

- Additionally, follow the 4R program above. Reducing inflammation isn't just about adding in anti-inflammatory foods and habits. It's also about removing the causes of inflammation.

- After the causes of inflammation have been removed, add in "anti-inflammatory" habits:

    o Proper sleep.

    o Exercise. Not too little, not too much.

    o Diet: remove food allergies and sensitivities (which you've already done with the 4R program)

- Manage stress
- Yes, these aren't covered in great depth in this book, but they are covered in my greater depth in my previous book, *STOP EXERCISING! The Way You Are Doing it Now.*

* And then, you can do the typical "anti-inflammatory diet":
  - Add in turmeric, ginger, cinnamon
  - Sprinkle in some lemon
  - Use apple cider vinegar where appropriate
  - Eat lots of green, leafy vegetables
  - Get enough omega 3s
  - Eat fruits, primary from the berry family (blueberries, strawberries, blackberries, etc.)

Supplements for Anxiety

While some supplements were mentioned earlier, we will elaborate on them in this section.

But before we do, I have to give the obligatory disclaimer: none of this is medical advice. I'm not a doctor. And I don't even play one on TV (even though my mom would like that). I don't know you, I haven't run tests on you, and I don't know what medications you are using. So before taking these, it's best to speak to a pharmacist. Yes, I emphasize a pharmacist and not a doctor. Typically, doctors have no training in nutritional supplements, so just to be conservative, they'll tell you not to take it, even though it may be beneficial. It's just hard for a doctor's ego to say "I don't know." But pharmacists do have training in supplements, so I would ask a pharmacist instead.

Also, keep in mind that supplements and medications do interact. There are 3 possible interactions:

1. The supplement makes the medication work better. This may result in an overdose.

2. The supplement makes the medication work worse, or ineffective.

3. The combination of the supplement and the medication creates side effects that independently, neither one does.

All the more reason to speak with a pharmacist before combining medications and supplements.

With that disclaimer out of the way, let's address supplements.

Magnesium

Multiple studies have found magnesium deficiency in people with anxiety. Additionally, more than one study has found that when people with anxiety supplement with magnesium, their anxiety decreases substantially[43, 44].

Most studies use magnesium sulfate, although one of the best forms of magnesium is magnesium glycinate. Typical doses are 300-1000 mg, although in some cases, higher doses may be safe, effective, and necessary.

Vitamin B Complex

Especially vitamins B6, B12 and folic acid are needed for the function of the nervous system. As they are water soluble, if you get too much, you just pee them out. With other nutrients, they could accumulate, so there is great safety in the B vitamins. It's still worth speaking to a pharmacist though before taking these vitamins, just to be on the safe side.

Kava

Kava is a herb that's considered to be a "natural benzodiazepine" (a class of drugs). There's a very good amount of research[45] behind kava, although most of it is relatively short in duration (to my knowledge, the longest study is around 6 months).

Some people taking kava report that it's "really strong" and it "numbs you."

Ashwagandha

Ashwagandha is a herb with decent evidence in reducing anxiety. The typical doses used are 300-500 mg/day.

Although there may be multiple mechanisms by which ashwagandha works, the most prevalent one seems to be a lowering of elevated cortisol.

Figure 31: **Supplements for Anxiety**

Magnesium   *Vitamin B Complex*   *Ashwagandha*   *Kava*

Nutrition for Depression

There are several nutritional links and causes to depression. This chapter will discuss those.

Thyroid

Just as with anxiety, a thyroid problem may actually be mistaken as depression if the thyroid is not tested properly.

The most common test for the thyroid is TSH. Sometimes, a T4 test will also be run. However, both of those are inadequate.

To get a complete picture of what's going on, you also want to run these tests:

- Free T3
- Free T4
- rT3 (that's reverse T3)
- TBG
- Anti-TPO antibodies
- Anti TGB antibodies (not to be confused with TBG)
- T3 Uptake

Of course, unless you know how to interpret these tests, the actual scores are meaningless, so make sure you work with someone skilled at interpretation.

But let's say you do discover that your thyroid is indeed slow. How should you eat to improve thyroid function?

A high-iodine diet would make sense if your thyroid is slow, but your results on the Anti-TPO and Anti-TGB antibodies came back as negative (a "negative" test means that the blood test came back with no elevations in those markers). However, the opposite is true if your antibodies are elevated – a low iodine diet makes more sense.

- Which foods contain high amounts of iodine?
    - Iodized salt
    - Most fish (especially cod)
    - Algae
    - Kale
    - Seaweed
    - Dairy
- Eat foods that are high in selenium, like:
    - Brazil nuts (6-8 nuts will do. Too much can be dangerous as well)
    - Pork

- Beef
- Turkey
- Eggs

And finally, gluten avoidance can also go a long way, which brings us to the next factor that can affect both your thyroid and your depression.

Figure 23: **Foods with high amounts of iodine**

Algae and seaweed   *Most fish*   *Iodized salt*   *Kale*

Figure 24: **Foods with high amounts of selenium**

Pork   *Beef*   *Turkey*   *Eggs*

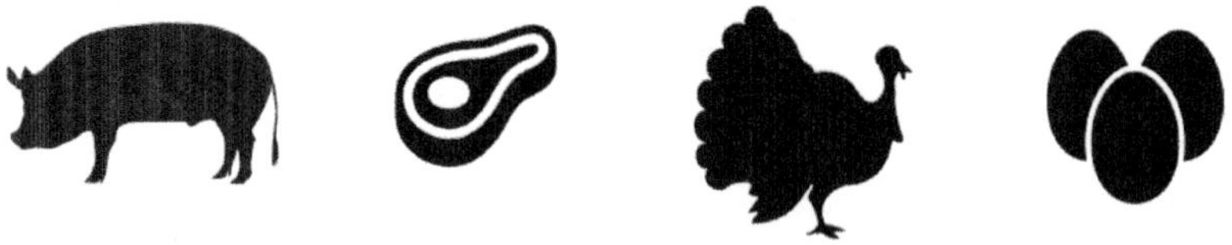

Low Blood Sugar

We covered this one in the section on anxiety, but it can also cause depression, albeit via different mechanisms.

Let's review:

In a healthy body, when someone consumes a carbohydrate-rich meal, blood sugar rises. When blood sugar rises, insulin also rises in order to bring blood sugar down, and sure enough, blood sugar steadily comes down to its pre-meal level (ideally 4.5-5.5 mmol/l) over a span of about 2 hours.

In someone who has low blood sugar (reactive hypoglycemia), one of 2 things happens (or both):

> 1. Blood sugar does come down to a normal level, but it happens too quickly. Instead of taking 2 hours to come down, it happens in 1 hour, or faster.

> 2. Blood sugar comes down below baseline, lower than 4.0 mmol/l.

And what happens when blood sugar goes too low? Since the body doesn't like things too high or too low, it takes certain measures to bring blood sugar back up. What are those measures? The release of certain hormones that bring blood sugar up: epinephrine (adrenaline), norepinephrine, growth hormone, glucagon, and the star of the show: cortisol. It's what they call in the media, "the stress hormone."

In someone with depression, cortisol tends to be higher than in someone who doesn't have depression.

Also, as a result of the hormonal milieu of low blood sugar, epinephrine, and norepinephrine can make it difficult to concentrate, and if it happens repeatedly, it can make a person tired.

How might you know if your depression is caused by low blood sugar? Here are a few clues:

- If your depression is worse right before meals
- If eating a meal relieves anxiety symptoms
- If you have a "crash" (increased depression), and eating sugar or something sweet relieves those symptoms

So it's quite important to be evaluated for your blood sugar if you have depression. One of the best tests to ask for is the oral glucose tolerance test (OGTT).

Figure 25: **Symptoms depression is caused by low blood sugar**

Worse right before meals and eating relieves symptoms

Sugar relieves symptoms

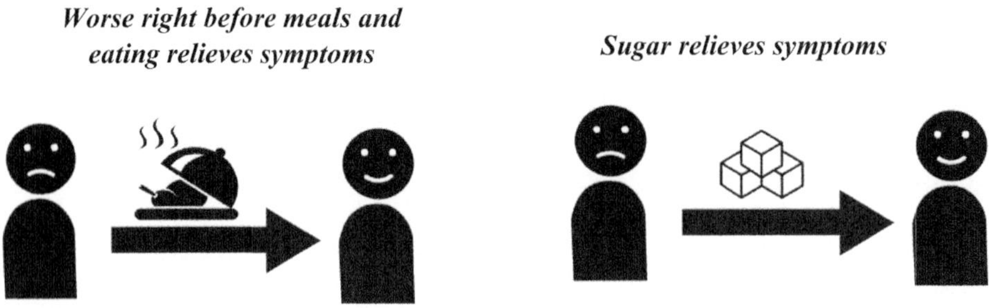

Food Sensitivities

Food sensitivities have been implicated in depression. In one study[46], participants with depression had improvements in their symptoms when they were put on a gluten-free diet. The group that did eat gluten did not improve. One more study[47] found the same thing.

One more general study[50] implicated food sensitivities in many different conditions.

The difference between a food allergy and sensitivity is simply this: if you have an allergy, the reaction is severe and immediate. If you have a food sensitivity the reaction is subtle and delayed. Our goal is to eliminate both from your diet. Although people tend to automatically eliminate foods to which they are allergic because of the symptoms that occur, rarely do we pay attention to food sensitivities. This is because the effects of the foods ingested are subtle and delayed (by hours to days) so we often do not make the connection with the delayed symptoms.

Some of these symptoms include nasal congestion a few hours after eating or an achy body the following day.

And it's not quite as obvious as "don't eat junk food or fast food." In fact, some otherwise healthy foods (like spinach, carrots, chicken, etc.) may be unhealthy for a specific person, and they would never suspect it, if it's a food they've been eating since they were a kid.

That's why it's worth finding out what you're sensitive to.

In order to investigate food sensitivities in my clients, I prefer to use a test that measure IgG, IgA, IgM and IgE which is a laboratory test that will accurately pinpoint food sensitivities. This test lists approximately 200 different foods.

If you prefer to not do the lab test, then you can go the route of doing an elimination diet. The downside of this option, although it may cost a lot less, is that you have to exercise self-discipline. To accurately find out what you are sensitive to, you *have* to eliminate the most common allergens for the four-week test period.

This means reading labels and being very careful about what you eat. That leaves you with plenty of vegetables (except for potatoes, tomatoes, bell peppers, egg plants,

corn, and chili peppers), most meats (except pork), and most nuts and seeds, in addition to all fruit. You can eat any of these in unlimited quantities. You should not go hungry—this is important.

If you have no time or patience for either option, eliminate the most common allergens in North America, which are gluten, dairy, sugar, corn, and soy. This is the least-preferred option out of the three because it is not specific to your body or its needs.

Intestinal Permeability

Strongly related to the previous section, on food sensitivities, intestinal permeability (sometimes called "leaky gut") has been implicated in numerous studies[48, 49, 50] when it comes to depression.

What is intestinal permeability? That is when the space between the cells of the small intestine is too wide. The small intestine should have space between the cells, but just small enough so that particles from the small intestine don't end up in the bloodstream. If that space is too wide, particles that are too large, which shouldn't be in the bloodstream, end up in the bloodstream.

Once it's in the bloodstream, the immune system detects those large particles as "foreign objects", and starts mounting an immune response to it.

To prevent that from happening, we need to "seal" the gut (small intestine). How do we do that? Using the 4R program that I've talked about in the chapter on nutrition for anxiety, as well as in my other book, *STOP EXERCISING! The Way You Are Doing it Now*. I'll re-print it below.

A common go-to is what's called the "4R program", popularized by Dr. Jeffrey ëBland.

It breaks down like this:

- Remove – infections, allergies, sensitivities

- Replace what's missing. Typically, that's stomach acid and enzymes

- Reinoculate – bring back the healthy bacteria that should be in your intestines in the first place

- Repair – the digestive lining. The layer that coats the stomach, to protect the walls of the stomach from the stomach acid.

Remove

First, you have to figure out what food sensitivities are keeping the inflammation cycle in your gut since that is yet another stress on the body.

The difference between a food allergy and sensitivity is simply this: if you have an allergy, the reaction is severe and immediate. If you have a food sensitivity the reaction is subtle and delayed. Our goal is to eliminate both from your diet. Although people tend to automatically eliminate foods to which they are allergic because of the symptoms that occur, rarely do we pay attention to food sensitivities. This is because the effects of the foods ingested are subtle and delayed (by hours to days) so we often do not make the connection with the delayed symptoms.

Some of these symptoms include nasal congestion a few hours after eating or achy body the following day.

In order to investigate food sensitivities in my clients, I prefer to use a test that measures IgG, IgA, IgM and IgE which is a laboratory test that accurately pinpoints food sensitivities. This test lists approximately 200 different foods.

If you prefer to not do the lab test, then you can go the route of doing an elimination diet. The downside of this option, although it may cost a lot less, is that you have to exercise self-discipline. To accurately find out what you are sensitive to, you *have* to eliminate the most common allergens for the four-week test period.

This means reading labels and being very careful about what you eat. That leaves you with plenty of vegetables (except for potatoes, tomatoes, bell peppers, egg plants,

corn, and chili peppers), most meats (except pork), and most nuts and seeds, in addition to all fruit. You can eat any of these in unlimited quantities. You should not go hungry -this is important.

If you have no time or patience for either option, eliminate the most common allergens in North America, which are gluten, dairy, sugar, corn, and soy. This is the least-preferred option out of the three because it is not specific to your body or its needs.

Replace

Replace that which was lost, such as digestive enzymes and restore stomach acid. Be sure to take high-quality digestive enzymes which help with the digestion of proteins, carbohydrates, and fats. These enzymes are protease, amylase, and lipase.

Reinoculate

Probiotics are friendly microorganisms that populate the small intestine, as we already discussed. You want to have more good bacteria in your gut than bad bacteria.

Most companies do not produce high-quality probiotics. Choose a capsule that has between 15 and 60-billion live bacteria in it.

Many think of yogurt as a good source of probiotics, but it contains an inadequate number to make much difference to your intestinal population. Choose a product that is guaranteed at the time of expiry, *not* at the date of manufacture and packaging, because some bacteria die off before you consume the capsules.

Different strains of bacteria have different lifespans. Companies who make high-quality probiotics compensate for the anticipated loss of bacteria in the time it takes the product to get to consumers. Additional bacteria are placed into the product to ensure a high number of bacteria survive to do their job in your intestines.

Check the product label for these very important words: "live and active cultures."

Additionally, eating foods that contain probiotics can be helpful. These foods include:

- Kefir
- Sauerkraut
- Yogurt
- Kimchi
- Kombucha

Prebiotics are the foods that probiotics eat! Feed those little guys what they need to survive and thrive. Prebiotics are found in bananas, honey, garlic, onions, and whole

grains. If a person is working on killing some bad bacteria and Candida, it's important to avoid fruits for a period of time (one to three weeks). So get your prebiotics through

supplements initially. Then you can switch to food sources.

Repair

It is essential that the lining of your digestive system is healthy. If there has been any damage, healing and repair need to take place before proper digestion and health can be maintained. The stomach has a coating around it which prevents it from being worn-out by the highly acidic hydrochloric acid, which can burn through a car hood if poured onto a car.

Glutamine helps to repair stomach lining. In addition to glutamine you can use DGL (*Deglycerrized* licorice) and aloe vera to repair the digestive lining.

In conclusion, it is essential to improve and maintain your digestive health. In taking steps to do so, you will reap the benefits and your body will thank you for it.

The Inflammation Connection

Just as inflammation plays a role in anxiety, it also plays a role in depression. To recap from the previous chapter:

We hear that word all the time – "inflammation." But what is it really? Inflammation is the immune system's response to a real or perceived threat. That response includes increased white blood cells (of which, there are many different subtypes), in order to identify and destroy the offending substance.

You might be thinking "inflammation is an issue of the immune system. What's the connection to a psychiatric condition, like depression?" I'll tell you.

One study[41] found inflammation to inhibit the parts of the brain called the "basal ganglia" and "cortical reward centre." These parts of the brain are responsible for motivation, learning, and a few other functions.

Interestingly enough, in one study[51], people who had depression, but didn't respond to antidepressants did better when those antidepressants were combined with anti-inflammatories (NSAIDs).

Now granted, correlation does not equal causation, but nonetheless, it's worth addressing inflammation in its own right.

What are the basics of reducing inflammation?

- Identify if there are any viruses, parasites, bacteria or fungi present in your body, which shouldn't be there. You'll need the help of a doctor for this. A basic complete blood count that looks at your white blood cells will give you a clue. A CDSA will give you even more precise results.

- Additionally, follow the 4R program above. Reducing inflammation isn't just about adding in anti-inflammatory foods and habits. It's also about removing the causes of inflammation.

- After the causes of inflammation have been removed, add in "anti-inflammatory" habits:

    o Proper sleep.

- Exercise. Not too little, not too much.
- Diet: remove food allergies and sensitivities (which you've already done with the 4R program)
- Manage stress
- Yes, these aren't covered in great depth in this book, but they are covered in my greater depth in my previous book, *STOP EXERCISING! The Way You Are Doing it Now.*

- And then, you can do the typical "anti-inflammatory diet":
  - Add in turmeric, ginger, cinnamon
  - Sprinkle in some lemon
  - Use apple cider vinegar where appropriate
  - Eat lots of green, leafy vegetables
  - Get enough omega 3s
  - Eat fruits, primary from the berry family (blueberries, strawberries, blackberries, etc.)

Alcohol

Sometimes we drink to drown out emotional pain, and sometimes, the opposite happens. We have no emotional pain, but the drinking leads to it.

Alcohol may cause depression via a couple of different mechanisms:

> 1. It may cause nutrient deficiencies (specifically B vitamins and magnesium). Vitamins B6, B12, and folic acid (also known as vitamin B9) are well-known nutrients necessary for good brain health.

> 2. It "slows down" the nervous system.

A word for warning though: if attempting to cut out alcohol cold-turkey, one of the withdrawal symptoms may actually be a worsening of the depression. It shouldn't last more than a few days, although granted – those will be a difficult few days, and feel longer than a few days.

Figure 33: **Consuming alcohol may cause depression**

Other Nutritional Factors in Depression

Although the research is weaker in these 2 areas, they're worth mentioning nonetheless:

Monosodium glutamate (MSG) is linked to depression, although, the majority of studies are in mice, rats, and monkeys.

Aspartame has slightly stronger research behind it. In one study[52], participants consumed a high-aspartame diet for 8 days. "High aspartame" is defined as 25 mg/kg/day. For a 70 kg (154-pound) person, that's about 10 cans of diet pop per day. In only 8 days, these participants experienced greater symptoms of depression.

So granted, these are not strong areas yet, but if you want to stack every factor in your favour, it may be worth removing MSG and aspartame from your diet.

Supplements

In case you didn't read the chapter on anxiety, I will give the same disclaimer here.

None of this is medical advice. I'm not a doctor. And I don't even play one on TV (even though my mom would like that). I don't know you, I haven't run tests on you, and I don't know what medications you are using. So before taking these, it's best to speak to a pharmacist. Yes, I emphasize a pharmacist and not a doctor. Typically, doctors have no training in nutritional supplements, so just to be conservative, they'll tell you not to take it, even though it may be beneficial. It's just hard for a doctor's ego to say "I don't know." But pharmacists do have training in supplements, so I would ask a pharmacist instead.

Also, keep in mind that supplements and medications do interact. There are 3 possible interactions:

1. The supplement makes the medication work better. This may result in an overdose.

2. The supplement makes the medication work worse, or ineffective.

3. The combination of the supplement and the medication creates side effects that independently, neither one does.

All the more reason to speak with a pharmacist before combining medications and supplements.

With that disclaimer out of the way, let's address supplements.

Zinc

Although zinc does not have antidepressant properties in and of itself, supplementation with zinc does enhance the effectiveness of other antidepressant therapies.

In one study[53], people for whom antidepressants didn't work were given zinc (25 mg/day), and in the 12 week period that the study was conducted, their depression improved a lot.

The results were replicated in a couple of other studies[54, 55].

Figure 34: **Supplementation with zinc may help with depression**

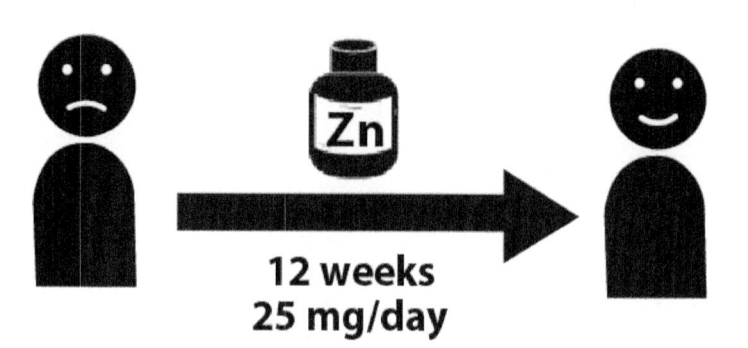

SAMe

Similar to zinc, some research shows that SAMe (s-adenosylmethionine) improves depression in those who are resistant to medications.

However, in addition to that, it has its own independent antidepressive effects.

Most of the time, the doses range from 400 mg, up to 1600 mg (400 mg, 4 times per day).

Inositol

Inositol is one of the B vitamins, although it's needed in much higher doses for the treatment of depression.

In one study[56], one group of participants was given 12 g/day of inositol, and their depression scores improved a lot more than those who were given a placebo.

It is also worthwhile noting that depression is often a symptom of vitamin B12 and folic acid deficiency, so it's certainly worth testing these (the gold standard test for B12 is actually called "methylmalonic acid", and not the standard "serum B12"). Once that deficiency is corrected, the depression goes away as well. So testing for these nutrients can be extremely valuable.

There is also research behind vitamin C, vitamin D, and other nutrients, that when they're deficient, improving nutrient status improves depression as well. But I do want to emphasize that point again – **when they're deficient**, supplementation helps. If they're not deficient, supplementation doesn't usually have much of an effect.

One of the best tests for nutrient status is the organic acids profile. Just what is an organic acids profile? Whenever we consume nutrients, we digest them, and change them into other chemicals. These chemicals are "residues" of the nutrients themselves. These "residues" are organic acids. They come out in the urine, and are a very strong indication of the body's nutrient status.

Conclusion and Quick Reference Guide

There you have it. You finally made it through this entire book. Although it's not the longest book in the world, it is at the time of this writing the most comprehensive book around on exercise for anxiety and depression. At the time of this writing, nothing else exists like it.

In this chapter, I'll simply summarize some of the big points from the different chapters.

Exercise Prescription for Anxiety

- 20-minutes of breathing exercises daily.
- 30 minutes of daily yoga practice
- Avoid high-intensity exercise with both cardio and strength training
- Intensity should be moderate (in the 50-70% range)
- Duration: 20 minutes
- Frequency: 3-4 times per week

- Maintain for a minimum of 16 weeks to see the best possible results

How to Exercise When It Feels Like a Panic Attack

- Warm up gradually. Take 5-10 minutes to warm up. Monitor your heart rate as you go through your warmup, to make sure it doesn't spike too quickly.
- Cool down gradually. Same guidelines as for a warmup.
- After a panic attack, reflect on it by actually writing it down on paper:
    - Did you die?
    - Was there physical pain?
- Exercise in a comfortable environment
    - Go to the gym during off-hours
    - Work with a personal trainer who makes you comfortable
- Distract yourself
- Take baby steps – exercise less than you think you can

Exercise Prescription for Depression

- Type: doesn't matter. Strength training and cardio work equally well

- Frequency: 3-5 times per week

- Intensity: high. For strength training: that's over 70% of your 1 repetition maximum (or approximately a weight that you can lift 12 times, but not 13). For cardio, high intensity is over 85% of your maximal heart rate

- Duration: 30 minutes or more

- How to adhere to exercise:

    o Do less than you think you can. If you think you can do 20 minutes, start with 10. In the early stages, positive momentum is more important than doing everything optimally.

    o Get an accountability partner

    o Get a personal trainer

    o Get a personal trainer who understands the principles in this book (not very many do)

Exercise for PTSD

- Type: all 3 major forms of exercise are effective – strength training, stretching, and cardio
- Duration: 30 minutes or more
- Frequency: 3 times per week or more

Mechanisms: Why Exercise Improves Mental Health

- Endorphins: pain-blocking hormones. They block not just physical pain, but emotional pain as well
- Self-efficacy hypothesis: feeling like you're in control of your situation
- Distraction hypothesis
- Sleep improvement
- Serotonin: increases in the amount of the "happy chemical" in the brain
- Brain wave optimization: balancing out the amount of alpha-to-beta waves
- Raising the anxiety threshold

Nutrition for Anxiety

- Get your thyroid properly tested. If your thyroid is not working properly, eat a low-iodine, high-selenium diet.

- Consider removing caffeine completely from the diet

- Consider removing aspartame from the diet

- Get tested for hypoglycemia (low blood sugar). If you do have low blood sugar, follow these recommendations:

    o Eat 4-6 smaller meals per day

    o Consume "slow" (low glycemic) carbohydrates. Choose things like beans, quinoa, buckwheat over things like potatoes, pasta, and rice

    o Avoid alcohol

    o Avoid refined sugar

    o Helpful supplements:

        - Chromium: 200-1000 mcg/day, in divided doses

        - L-Carnitine: 500-2000 mg/day

        - B complex vitamins

- Improve digestive function using the 4R program

- Helpful supplements if low blood sugar is <u>not</u> the issue:
    - Magnesium glycinate: 300-1000 mg/day
    - Vitamin B complex
    - Kava
    - Ashwagandha

Nutrition for Depression

- Get proper thyroid testing. If your thyroid is not working properly, eat a low-iodine, high-selenium diet.
- Get tested for hypoglycemia (low blood sugar). If you do have low blood sugar, follow these recommendations:
    - Eat 4-6 smaller meals per day
    - Consume "slow" (low glycemic) carbohydrates. Choose things like beans, quinoa, buckwheat over things like potatoes, pasta, and rice
    - Avoid alcohol
    - Avoid refined sugar
    - Helpful supplements:

- Chromium: 200-1000 mcg/day, in divided doses
             - L-Carnitine: 500-2000 mg/day
             - B complex vitamins
- Get tested for food sensitivities, and remove them.
- Avoid alcohol
- Consider removing aspartame and MSG
- Helpful supplements:
    - Zinc: 25 mg/day
    - SAMe: 400-1600 mg/day
    - Inositol: 12 g/day
- Get tested for vitamin B12 and folic acid. Often deficiencies in these nutrients lead to depression
- Consider running a test called an "organic acids profile" – this tells you your nutrient deficiencies

References

1. Katzman MA, Vermani M, Gerbarg PL, et al. A multicomponent yoga-based, breath intervention program as an adjunctive treatment in patients suffering from generalized anxiety disorder with or without comorbidities. Int J Yoga. 2012;5(1):57-65.

2. Doria S, De vuono A, Sanlorenzo R, Irtelli F, Mencacci C. Anti-anxiety efficacy of Sudarshan Kriya Yoga in general anxiety disorder: A multicomponent, yoga based, breath intervention program for patients suffering from generalized anxiety disorder with or without comorbidities. J Affect Disord. 2015;184:310-7.

3. Hale BS, Raglin JS. State anxiety responses to acute resistance training and step aerobic exercise across eight weeks of training. J Sports Med Phys Fitness. 2002;42(1):108-12.

4. Herring MP, Jacob ML, Suveg C, Dishman RK, O'connor PJ. Feasibility of exercise training for the short-term treatment of generalized anxiety disorder: a randomized controlled trial. Psychother Psychosom. 2012;81(1):21-8.

5. Raglin JS, Turner PE, Eksten F. State anxiety and blood pressure following 30 min of leg ergometry or weight training. Med Sci Sports Exerc. 1993;25(9):1044-8.

6. Tsutsumi T, Don BM, Zaichkowsky LD, Delizonna LL. Physical fitness and psychological benefits of strength training in community dwelling older adults. Appl Human Sci. 1997;16(6):257-66.

7. Strickland JC, Smith MA. The anxiolytic effects of resistance exercise. Front Psychol. 2014;5:753.

8. O'connor PJ, Cook DB. Anxiolytic and blood pressure effects of acute static compared to dynamic exercise. Int J Sports Med. 1998;19(3):188-92.

9. Sjögren T, Nissinen KJ, Järvenpää SK, Ojanen MT, Vanharanta H, Mälkiä EA. Effects of a physical exercise intervention on subjective physical well-being, psychosocial functioning and general well-being among office workers: a cluster randomized-controlled cross-over design. Scand J Med Sci Sports. 2006;16(6):381-90.

10. Norvell N, Belles D. Psychological and physical benefits of circuit weight training in law enforcement personnel. J Consult Clin Psychol. 1993;61(3):520-7.

11. Asmundson GJ, Fetzner MG, Deboer LB, Powers MB, Otto MW, Smits JA. Let's get physical: a contemporary review of the anxiolytic effects of exercise for anxiety and its disorders. Depress Anxiety. 2013;30(4):362-73.

12. Wipfli BM, Rethorst CD, Landers DM. The anxiolytic effects of exercise: a meta-analysis of randomized trials and dose-response analysis. J Sport Exerc Psychol. 2008;30(4):392-410.

13. Stubbs B, Vancampfort D, Rosenbaum S, et al. An examination of the anxiolytic effects of exercise for people with anxiety and stress-related disorders: A meta-analysis. Psychiatry Res. 2017;249:102-108.

14. Stubbs B, Vancampfort D, Rosenbaum S, et al. An examination of the anxiolytic effects of exercise for people with anxiety and stress-related disorders: A meta-analysis. Psychiatry Res. 2017;249:102-108.

15. Young SN. How to increase serotonin in the human brain without drugs. J Psychiatry Neurosci. 2007;32(6):394-9.

16. https://www.fitnesssolutionsplus.ca/blog/measurements/

17. Doyne EJ, Ossip-klein DJ, Bowman ED, Osborn KM, Mcdougall-wilson IB, Neimeyer RA. Running versus weight lifting in the treatment of depression. J Consult Clin Psychol. 1987;55(5):748-54.

18. Martinsen EW, Hoffart A, Solberg O. Comparing aerobic with nonaerobic forms of exercise in the treatment of clinical depression: a randomized trial. Compr Psychiatry. 1989;30(4):324-31.

19. Singh NA, Clements KM, Fiatarone MA. A randomized controlled trial of progressive resistance training in depressed elders. J Gerontol A Biol Sci Med Sci. 1997;52(1):M27-35.

20. Dunn AL, Trivedi MH, Kampert JB, Clark CG, Chambliss HO. Exercise treatment for depression: efficacy and dose response. Am J Prev Med. 2005;28(1):1-8.

21. Singh NA, Stavrinos TM, Scarbek Y, Galambos G, Liber C, Fiatarone singh MA. A randomized controlled trial of high versus low intensity weight training versus general practitioner care for clinical depression in older adults. J Gerontol A Biol Sci Med Sci. 2005;60(6):768-76.

22. Noh JW, Lee SA, Choi HJ, Hong JH, Kim MH, Kwon YD. Relationship between the intensity of physical activity and depressive symptoms among Korean adults: analysis of Korea Health Panel data. J Phys Ther Sci. 2015;27(4):1233-7.

23. Singh NA, Clements KM, Fiatarone MA. A randomized controlled trial of progressive resistance training in depressed elders. J Gerontol A Biol Sci Med Sci. 1997;52(1):M27-35.

24. Craft LL, Perna FM. The Benefits of Exercise for the Clinically Depressed. Prim Care Companion J Clin Psychiatry. 2004;6(3):104-111.

25. Craft LL, Perna FM. The Benefits of Exercise for the Clinically Depressed. Prim Care Companion J Clin Psychiatry. 2004;6(3):104-111.

26. Netz Y. Is the Comparison between Exercise and Pharmacologic Treatment of Depression in the Clinical Practice Guideline of the American College of Physicians Evidence-Based?. Front Pharmacol. 2017;8:257.American Journal of Preventive Medicine. 2005 Jan;28(1):1-8

27. Rosenbaum S, Sherrington C, Tiedemann A. Exercise augmentation compared with usual care for post-traumatic stress disorder: a randomized controlled trial. Acta Psychiatr Scand. 2015;131(5):350-9.

28. Shivakumar G, Anderson EH, Surís AM, North CS. Exercise for PTSD in Women Veterans: A Proof-of-Concept Study. Mil Med. 2017;182(11):e1809-e1814.

29. Kim SH, Schneider SM, Bevans M, et al. PTSD symptom reduction with mindfulness-based stretching and deep breathing exercise: randomized controlled clinical trial of efficacy. J Clin Endocrinol Metab. 2013;98(7):2984-92.

30. Greden JF. Anxiety or caffeinism: a diagnostic dilemma. Am J Psychiatry. 1974;131(10):1089-92.

31. Uhde TW, Boulenger JP, Jimerson DC, Post RM. Caffeine: relationship to human anxiety, plasma MHPG and cortisol. Psychopharmacol Bull. 1984;20(3):426-30.

32. Uhde TW, Boulenger JP, Jimerson DC, Post RM. Caffeine: relationship to human anxiety, plasma MHPG and cortisol. Psychopharmacol Bull. 1984;20(3):426-30.

33. De freitas B, Schwartz G. Effects of caffeine in chronic psychiatric patients. Am J Psychiatry. 1979;136(10):1337-8.

34. De freitas B, Schwartz G. Effects of caffeine in chronic psychiatric patients. Am J Psychiatry. 1979;136(10):1337-8.

35. Choudhary AK, Lee YY. Neurophysiological symptoms and aspartame: What is the connection?. Nutr Neurosci. 2018;21(5):306-316.

36. Roberts, H.J.. (1988). Reactions attributed to aspartame-containing products: 551 cases. Journal of Applied Nutrition. 40. 85-94.

37. Markle JG, Frank DN, Mortin-toth S, et al. Sex differences in the gut microbiome drive hormone-dependent regulation of autoimmunity. Science. 2013;339(6123):1084-8.

38. Bonaz B, Bazin T, Pellissier S. The Vagus Nerve at the Interface of the Microbiota-Gut-Brain Axis. Front Neurosci. 2018;12:49.

39. Lach G, Schellekens H, Dinan TG, Cryan JF. Anxiety, Depression, and the Microbiome: A Role for Gut Peptides. Neurotherapeutics. 2018;15(1):36-59.

40. Busby E, Bold J, Fellows L, Rostami K. Mood Disorders and Gluten: It's Not All in Your Mind! A Systematic Review with Meta-Analysis. Nutrients. 2018;10(11)

41. Felger JC. Imaging the Role of Inflammation in Mood and Anxiety-related Disorders. Curr Neuropharmacol. 2018;16(5):533-558.

42. Pierce GL, Kalil GZ, Ajibewa T, et al. Anxiety independently contributes to elevated inflammation in humans with obesity. Obesity (Silver Spring). 2017;25(2):286-289.

43. De souza MC, Walker AF, Robinson PA, Bolland K. A synergistic effect of a daily supplement for 1 month of 200 mg magnesium plus 50 mg vitamin B6 for the relief of anxiety-related premenstrual symptoms: a randomized, double-blind, crossover study. J Womens Health Gend Based Med. 2000;9(2):131-9.

44. Iannello S, Belfiore F. Hypomagnesemia. A review of pathophysiological, clinical and therapeutical aspects. Panminerva Med. 2001;43(3):177-209.

45. Volz HP, Kieser M. Kava-kava extract WS 1490 versus placebo in anxiety disorders--a randomized placebo-controlled 25-week outpatient trial. Pharmacopsychiatry. 1997;30(1):1-5.

46. Peters SL, Biesiekierski JR, Yelland GW, Muir JG, Gibson PR. Randomised clinical trial: gluten may cause depression in subjects with non-coeliac gluten sensitivity - an exploratory clinical study. Aliment Pharmacol Ther. 2014;39(10):1104-12.

47. Carr AC. Depressed mood associated with gluten sensitivity--resolution of symptoms with a gluten-free diet. N Z Med J. 2012;125(1366):81-2.

48. Shor RE, Cobb JC. An exploratory study of hypnotic training using the concept of plateau responsiveness as a referent. Am J Clin Hypn. 1968;10(3):178-93.

49. Bischoff SC, Barbara G, Buurman W, et al. Intestinal permeability--a new target for disease prevention and therapy. BMC Gastroenterol. 2014;14:189.

50. Cryan JF, Dinan TG. Mind-altering microorganisms: the impact of the gut microbiota on brain and behaviour. Nat Rev Neurosci. 2012;13(10):701-12.

51. Touraine R. [Pseudoxanthoma elasticum or systematized elastorrhexia (recent concepts)]. Acquis Med Recent. 1967;:123-41.

52. Lindseth GN, Coolahan SE, Petros TV, Lindseth PD. Neurobehavioral effects of aspartame consumption. Res Nurs Health. 2014;37(3):185-93.

53. Siwek M, Dudek D, Paul IA, et al. Zinc supplementation augments efficacy of imipramine in treatment resistant patients: a double blind, placebo-controlled study. J Affect Disord. 2009;118(1-3):187-95.

54. Ranjbar E, Shams J, Sabetkasaei M, et al. Effects of zinc supplementation on efficacy of antidepressant therapy, inflammatory cytokines, and brain-derived neurotrophic factor in patients with major depression. Nutr Neurosci. 2014;17(2):65-71.

55. Nowak G, Siwek M, Dudek D, Zieba A, Pilc A. Effect of zinc supplementation on antidepressant therapy in unipolar depression: a preliminary placebo-controlled study. Pol J Pharmacol. 2003;55(6):1143-7.

56. Levine J, Barak Y, Gonzalves M, et al. Double-blind, controlled trial of inositol treatment of depression. Am J Psychiatry. 1995;152(5):792-4.

Printed in Great Britain
by Amazon